Henry Morris:

Village Colleges, Community Education and the Ideal Order

by Tony Jeffs

The Educational Heretics Series

Published 1998 by Educational Heretics Press
113 Arundel Drive, Bramcote Hills Nottingham NG9 3FQ

British Cataloguing in Publication Data

A catalogue record for this book is available from the British Library

Jeffs, Tony

Henry Morris: Village Colleges, Community Education and the Ideal Order

ISBN 1-900219-06-9

Design and production: Educational Heretics Press

Printed by Mastaprint, Sandiacre, Nottinghamshire

Contents

Full lasting is the song, though he
The singer passes; lasting too
For souls not lent in usury
The rapture of the forward view

"The Thrush in February"
George Meredith (1828-1909)

Plaque in the entrance of Impington Village College

Henry Morris
by George Robson

Acknowledgements

Too many individuals contributed to this short book to attempt a list without offending those overlooked due to poor record-keeping. Suffice it to say an all-embracing thank you at this late stage to those who willingly discussed Henry Morris and the Village Colleges with me. Indulging my enthusiasm was probably not always easy. Especially for my Durham University colleagues Sarah Banks and Umme Imam who endured the ramblings whilst helping me find the time and space for research. To Ruth Gilchrist for reading the manuscript, spotting mistakes and locating excesses. Much of the thinking, as always, originated from joint work with Mark Smith. Thankfully he alone will recognise where this occurs and discretion regarding these matters has always been an endearing characteristic. Finally to Jackie Apperley for suggesting improvements and sustaining an interest in Henry Morris for almost as long as I have.

A special thank you to Rose Swannell who kindly agreed to be interviewed and loaned me the tape of a splendid programme on Henry Morris made by her husband Edwin Swannell, who prior to retirement was Warden of Linton Village College. Also to David Farnell who many years ago allowed me to photocopy his excellent but sadly unpublished study of Morris. Perhaps he will be persuaded to eventually publish it.

This book forms part of a series on individuals who helped create and sustain a vision of what education can achieve when the deadhand of those merely concerned with training the young and managing society is loosened. Roland Meighan's industry, editorial skills and sheer tenacity in driving those he commissions to complete deserves recognition and gratitude. Roland certainly gets mine in abundance.

Introduction

Henry Morris's name is invariably linked with the Cambridgeshire Village Colleges he, more than anyone, helped create. Reflecting on them it becomes clear they were one of the most remarkable educational achievements of the century. Cambridgeshire Village Colleges still, over three-quarters of a century after Morris first drafted the blueprint, embody a vision of education, which remains breath-taking in its audacity and ingenuity. From their inception they were designed to be more than a new type of school, a variation on a well rehearsed theme. Morris was determined to '*do away with the insulated school*' (1926: 39), by devising an institution offering a rounded education for young people of school-age whilst simultaneously providing a cultural, leisure and social centre for the whole community. Beautiful places which would mature into '*centres of corporate life and not congeries of classrooms for discourse and instruction*' (op cit).

Harry Ree his principal biographer claims at various points that Henry 'started Community Education', 'was the first to put forward a workable scheme for lifelong education', was 'the beggetter of the community school' and initiated the 'democratisation of education through extending control to the community'. Regretfully this is an exaggerated account of his contribution. Morris did not invent the community school, community education or lifelong education as many besides Ree have suggested. These like many equally extravagant claims made on his behalf are misleading. But with regards all three he may, in Britain at least, have done more to prove their viability, to thwart the glib denunciations of those seeking to dismiss each as utopian figments of a radical imagination than anyone else. Morris built in the most inauspicious circumstances institutions which if opened today would be heralded as innovative precursors of an educational future worthy of the twenty-first century. Yet the politicians and their cronies attending the grand media launch, jostling for a sound bite and scattering quotes and press-notices in every direction are unlikely to have heard of Morris or deliberated on his ideas. Languishing somewhat forgotten Morris is an educational prophet who like Robert Owen, Holmes or Dewey remains a mite too critical and overly iconoclastic for the palate of contemporary educational planners and policy-makers. Attacks he launched decades ago on centralised planning, an imposed national curriculum and traditional teaching methods still possess the bite to make those currently in charge of the education system wince. Reading Morris today for those enamoured with the ever-quickening drift towards a system characterised by the inter-weaving of new technology, new managerialism and unadulterated old style authoritarianism is a chastening encounter. Repeatedly one is obliged to reflect on the volume of change endured for such paucity of progress. How there is no inevitably about educational progress and the tenuous hold of so many of the 'advances' achieved.

Reading Morris is not a Herculean labour. An accomplished writer his output was bewilderingly meagre for someone who had once been a working journalist. His only substantial work, comprising little over 8,000 words, is the ponderously titled **The Village College: Being a Memorandum on the Provision of Educational and Social Facilities for the Countryside, with Special Reference to Cambridgeshire.** Routinely referred to as the Memorandum even this was a self-funded publication written in 1924 just four years after leaving university. The residue comprises a mix of conference papers, transcripts of radio broadcasts, a book review, the odd article, a lone book chapter and briefing papers. Most of this motley collection is to be found in a slim volume entitled **The Henry Morris Collection** edited by Harry Ree (1984).

I never met Henry Morris but have spoken to many who did. Some knew him well, most liked him, some did not.

Without exception all communicated an undiminished admiration for his breadth of vision and intellect.

My initial encounters with Morris occurred over thirty years ago whilst working as a neophyte community education tutor in Leicestershire. The name seemed to crop up whenever the more interesting and committed senior colleagues mused on the meaning of community education. One even recounted tales of working in Cambridgeshire during Morris's final years as Director of Education. Rashly I then concluded Morris was not someone I would have liked, or wished to work with. Subsequent conversations with others who knew him have led me to unreservedly amend this verdict. Similarly over time the more I have read by and about him so my admiration has burgeoned.

Given a scholarly yet readable biography exists every attempt has been made to avoid replication. However despite seeking to concentrate on the ideas and achievements rather than the life story duplication was inescapable. How could it be otherwise? Hopefully this text will compliment Ree's and thereby encourage those familiar with it to re-visit and the unacquainted to seek it out.

Chapter One

Roots and routes

Morris was born in Southport, Lancashire in 1889. His mother died when he was twelve and his father was a plumber. He spoke little of his family. Indeed so rare were the references that any which occurred remained fixed in the memory of colleagues. One who worked closely with him for many years recalled his mother being mentioned only once. This was when an elderly clerk who questioned his judgement was warned to beware his temper because '*my Mother was pure Irish*'. The clerk not to be bested replied '*that explains a lot sir*'. Southport today has proportionately more people aged 60 and over than anywhere else in England. Things were not markedly different when Morris and his seven brothers and sisters grew up there. Southport then, as now, was somewhere you went for a quiet seaside holiday or tranquil retirement. If we know little of those early years this is largely because Morris decided it should be so. Indeed not only was the topic of his childhood and family evaded but on occasions the curious were fed false information.

The bare facts are these. Morris left school at fourteen, worked for **The Southport Visitor**, a local paper, and rapidly progressed from office boy to reporter. Outside work his life appears to have centred on the local Anglican church and the Harris Institute at Preston. Part-time study at the Institute eventually led in 1910 to a place at St David's University College, Lampeter. Aged 21 he enrolled to read Theology with the clear intention of becoming a Church of England minister.

The university years

It was a somewhat chequered and staccato university career lasting nine years. He left St David's after two years in dramatic circumstances. Following a solitary refusal to sign a petition circulated within the College opposing the proposed Disestablishment of the Church of Wales. An altercation with the other students ensued, writs flew hither and thither and heated exchanges in the local press transpired. Although the details are sparse Morris's unwillingness to sign, despite intense pressure gave every indication of a future determination not to flinch from taking an unpopular stance when the need arose. From Lampeter he transferred to Exeter College, Oxford where he remained prior to enlisting in the army in November 1914. Demobbed in 1919 Theology was rapidly abandoned along with all intentions of entering the Church and returning to Oxford. Relocating to King's College Cambridge he read philosophy graduating in 1920.

One mystery which surrounded this period was who funded or at least underwrote his education. Amongst colleagues rumours circulated of a rich older woman who 'adopted' Henry. Mention was also made of a kindly clergyman who 'helped out'. Hard evidence of their existence was never forthcoming. Without sponsorship someone from his background would have found it difficult, but not impossible, to survive. However according to van der Eyken and Turner (1969) the truth is much more mundane. Morris it seems was funded throughout by his family but lacked the good grace to allot them the credit preferring grandiloquent rumours of wealthy benefactors to circulate unchecked.

By the 1920s Morris was describing himself as a Socialist but it was a somewhat idiosyncratic self-wrought variety. Albeit at times close to the Labour Party, the suspicion lingers that contacts were made and proximity sought for pragmatic rather than ideological reasons. Important exceptions to this should be noted especially David Hardman a longstanding supporter and friend. First a Labour Councillor on the Cambridgeshire County Council, then a Parliamentary Private Secretary in the 1945-51 Labour government and finally secretary of the Cassel Educational Trust which helped fund the Digswell project Morris launched following retirement. Hardman, a don and writer, linked to a range of good causes was typical of the Left leaning, progressive and culturally aware set Morris consistently orientated towards. Morris was also a resolute democrat with scant patience or respect for most local or national politicians. Much as he was an egalitarian repelled by mass culture who arranged a compartmentalised life which ensured leisure time was shared with others who likewise embraced 'high culture'. Amongst Oxford and Cambridge alumni of his generation a small but significant number migrated, or perhaps more accurately drifted, into the Social Democratic and Fabian camp post-1918. Many, like Morris, had also initially been aligned to a philosophical movement usually categorised as British Idealism. During his time at Oxford Idealism lost much of its earlier omnipotence but nevertheless remained influential. Idealism moulded his educational thinking and aspirations much as it had that of other progressive educators of the period such as Dewey, Holmes and Sadler. To a large extent he never relinquished his adherence to this tradition perhaps initially acquired from his Oxford tutor.

Henry's Oxford tutor was the cleric, theologian, historian and philosopher Hastings Rashdall. Now remembered, if at all, as the author of a three volume history of the European universities in the Middle Ages. They remained in regular contact from their first meeting up until Rashdall's death in 1924. Rashdall was one of the few individuals Morris acknowledged as an influence on his educational thinking and according to a friend remained a hero who Henry never tired of quoting (Palmer 1976: 243).

This friendship was important to Morris. Perhaps more significant than the personal relationship was the extent to which Rashdall nurtured his intellectual development and faith in the value of education. When Morris arrived at Oxford T H Green, the central figure of the Idealist movement who spent all his adult life in Oxford, had been dead for three decades. Followers, prominent amongst whom was Rashdall, however retained immense influence.

Many undertook to sustain the tradition of scholarship married to public service which Green, along with others such as Jowett and Toynbee, had promoted.

Rashdall, via example as much as tutelage, equipped Morris with a set of philosophical ideas upon which his educational theories were built. His tutor was a redoubtable campaigner for educational reform. He was an active supporter of the WEA from its establishment in 1903; a man who, as his correspondence reveals, derived great fulfilment from firsthand involvement in adult education. At Oxford he taught extension classes, and subsequently as Dean of Durham and Carlisle Cathedral devoted his spare time to teaching adult classes. Rashdall also wrote on educational matters. His most famous book **The Universities of Europe in the Middle Ages** (1895) attracted considerable attention when it appeared and remains a seminal history. Over a century later it is difficult to grasp why a lengthy tome on an obscure topic precipitated such a stir; two reasons in particular explain this.

The first relates to long-standing debates regarding the desirability, or otherwise, of expanding the number of universities. And, if so, whether the subjects and disciplines taught should be augmented along with student numbers. Then, as now, traditionalists were convinced more, subjects and students alike, meant worse. New disciplines it was argued, expressly those linked to trade and commerce, would devalue scholarship and the standing of universities. Rashdall's work seriously undermined this position by demonstrating how the very universities critics of expansion now fought 'to protect' had previously taught both universal and vocational knowledge. By implication he queried if having once taught Astronomy to assist navigators why now resist engineering for shipbuilders. Morris subsequently viewed divisions between vocational and academic subjects as artificial and damaging. Indeed it was a central tenet of the Village Colleges that they should eradicate such segmentation. Rashdall, like his pupil, was never a narrow vocationalist displaying scant sympathy for the College of Commerce model of Further and Higher education. He would certainly be contemptuous of the narrow vocationalism of NVQs and 'employer led' training schemes currently in vogue. Rashdall passionately believed that vocationally orientated students should be inducted into the theory under-pinning their craft. For without such an initiation they would be consigned the role of operative. Equally they should enjoy access to a '*liberal or general education*' (Rashdall 1902: 69). For, like Ruskin and William Morris, he held that industry without art led to barbarism.

The second reason was the implicit textual message. Published when Victorians were struggling to understand and accommodate what many perceived as unprecedented change, it provided grounds for optimism regarding the future. Around them '*all that was solid was melting into thin air*'. Industrialisation and urbanisation transformed beyond recognition the appearance of town and country; induced unprecedented population growth, which Malthusians told them threatened the destruction of civilisation and human survival; swept away 'Merrie England' along with a rural way of life which had seemingly survived for centuries; and obliterated social customs and religious, scientific and political beliefs once assumed eternal. Rashdall's history recounts the story of a time when coincidentally civilisation also appeared threatened, even doomed. When barbarism was rampant; robber barons and tyrants held sway; and culture, morality and social equilibrium were judged to be in wholesale retreat. Readers though surprisingly encountered an encouraging not disheartening narrative. Detailing how isolated seats of learning scattered across Europe managed against enormous odds to preserve and protect so much that was good and worthwhile. Thereby establishing the foundations for the better, more rational and humane society. Many, Morris included, found Rashdall's work inspirational and comforting. Educational institutions it seemed, when they were founded on sound principles, clearly had the capacity to protect the best of the past whilst nurturing a superior world. Even in the most inauspicious of circumstances.

Rashdall's enthusiasm for educational and social reform reflected his religious and political beliefs. Like many of his background and generation he was a neo-Hegelian, an affiliate of the philosophical movement known as British Idealism. T H Green, Rashdall tells us, was one of the two writers to whom he owed his greatest debt. John Dewey, possibly the most renowned American advocate of the community school, acknowledged a similar obligation.

Morris was very much a product of the Idealist tradition, adopting the core tenets in his youth he spent the rest of his life endeavouring to apply them. Believing like all British Idealists that the transformation of society and the promotion of the '*good life*' depended as much on changing the moral attitudes of citizens as upon governmental reforms. Active citizenship, linked to the building of vibrant communities, were central to this doctrine. Energetic campaigners for universal suffrage from the onset, Idealists held that citizenship required far more of the individual than an obligation to cast their votes once a year. Rather citizenship imposed on all, the obligation to '*cultivate*' their '*best self*' and pursue the '*common good*'. Because, as Green explained, the individual '*bettered himself through institutions and habits which tend to make the welfare of all the welfare of each*' (quoted Nettleship 1888: cxxxviii). Green, like Rashdall, was a devout Christian who according to an early biographer '*held the life of citizenship to be a mode of divine service*' (MacCunn 1907: 220). Faith in God was not a pre-requisite for affiliation as Morris and others subsequently demonstrated. Recognition that the individual might only realize their best self in community with others was. Idealists saw '*an automatic relationship between fulfilling one's capacities and taking on a responsible role in society*' (Vincent and Plant 1984:27). As Morris explained '*it is as members of a community that the life of action and conduct is best realized and our souls saved*' (1926: 35). Within Idealism is encountered an attempt to reconcile the twin ideals of community and freedom; to walk a tightrope betwixt communitarianism and individualism. Like all Hegelians and Neo-Hegelians Idealists refused to tolerate dualisms. They struggled to find unifying doctrines and solutions to seemingly irreconcilable conflicts. Social harmony, amidst change and confusion, could be found it seems when the individual willed and strived for what Green termed the '*common good*'. Unquestioning altruism was not demanded for individuals would be committed to achieving this end once convinced they could only fully realise themselves within a community of equals. Freedom after all acquired meaning only within the context of the living community. Collective action and association were essential to give freedom meaning and because they would enable poverty, ignorance and unemployment to be vanquished. As Green explains all citizens

> *ought to be called upon to do that as a body which under the conditions of modern life cannot be done if everyone is left to himself.* (1888: 432)

Or as a follower explained in language with an extraordinary contemporary ring to it '*the power of the good state empowers the citizen, and the power of the good citizen empowers the state*' (Jones 1919: 89).

Idealists saw involvement in the work of School Boards and other educational organizations as being of the highest priority. After all education was the route by which '*the ideal order and the actual order can ultimately be made one*' (Morris 1925: 17). Accessible free education irrespective of age or status was essential, Green argued, because those denied knowledge were excluded from full citizenship, marginalised. Until a '*freemasonry of common education*' (1888: 460) existed society would inevitably be divided into ruled and rulers and class antagonism remain entrenched. Green, therefore, advocated elementary schools that catered for all living in a neighbourhood. Believing like Morris the case against private education was a moral one. For if the wealthy were allowed to withdraw their children from the 'community school' then Britain would be '*riven into two nations, not on any principle based on virtue or intelligence but on money*' (Morris 1941: 63). Today when the Labour and Liberal parties are too terrified to discuss, let alone propose, reform of the Public School system it is tempting to dismiss

baths, people's theatres and assembly rooms. Their task was to revive '*the neighborly spirit, the democracy that we knew before we came to the city*' (quoted Perry 1910: 270). Unfortunately a new administration cut funding and curtailed the experiment but Ward continued to champion them at conferences and meetings across America. So successfully that all three Presidential candidates in the 1912 election endorsed school social centers as a key reform. Rochester may have gone but by 1921 Woods (1923) reports 170 cities had school centers many employing full-time community organisers to undertake outreach and developmental work (Gluek 1927).

Whitehouse during this period promoted similar developments in Britain. Calling for schools in urban areas to be grouped together and set within parkland alongside swimming baths, gymnasiums, restaurants, library, concert and art rooms to be shared by schools and community. Carson (1990) notes by the 1900s in America settlement workers had joined progressive educationalists in criticising the antediluvian restrictions of the formal education curriculum that segregated the vocational and academic. Advocating as Morris did in the Memorandum an institution providing '*for the whole man*' where '*life is lived*' and the '*dismal dispute*' between vocational and non-vocational education would be rendered irrelevant.

Clear differences between Village Colleges and settlements must be noted. First, until the coalfield settlements appeared in the 1930s, the latter were invariably located in urban settings where it was assumed poverty was more acute and the breakdown of community more pronounced. Second, settlements were established by voluntary groups who typically shared an attachment to a particular university or public school. Finally, settlements never provided full-time schooling. These differences should not be allowed to obscure the similarities. For what Morris hoped to create was a network of rural school-based settlements fostering fellowship, association, neighbourliness and a sense of community. Capable of converting society into a series of cultural communities, where every local community would become an education society, and education would not merely be a consequence of good government, but good government a consequence of education. Like Ward and Simkhovitch he wanted a new type of school but never acknowledged their contribution or indeed that of any others. Maybe Morris never encountered the English advocates of school social centres such as Sadler or Haldane, nor read the literature; or perhaps opted to ignore them - who knows? Sadly though as a result an important educational innovation has been totally ignored here and the credit for 'inventing' the community school exclusively bestowed by English commentators on Henry Morris.

War and the route to Cambridgeshire

Like so many others Morris cut short his education to enlist following the outbreak of war. Unlike the majority who left Oxford in 1914 to enlist he returned. War inevitably changed Morris. At a time when so few entered higher education Morris was destined for a commission. Gazetted to the Royal Army Service Corp he eventually became a Captain and was mentioned in dispatches. Service in France and Italy offered an opportunity to acquire administrative and managerial skills, but these were procured at a dreadful price. He saw action, witnessed terrible carnage and lost friends and faith alike. De-mobbed in 1919 he returned to Oxford but it proved a fleeting sojourn. Rashdall had departed first to Hereford, then Durham and eventually Carlisle where after brief service as Dean he died. Studying Theology probably seemed fatuous having abandoned his faith along with any desire to enter the Church; he quit Oxford unable to endure the memories of '*the golden hours there years ago, and all my dear friends ... killed in the war*' (letter quoted Ree 1973: 10). Henry transferred to Cambridge where he was to live for all but eight of the following 42 years.

Military service had it's compensations. Morris returned to Civvie Street with a new persona. During the war he cultivated the mannerisms, elan and accent of the Public School officers with whom he shared the Mess. All traces of a Lancashire twang, along with the deference expected of a

Board school boy were jettisoned. Henceforth, as the wife of a colleague, recounts he was '*tall handsome and striking ... with the military bearing of a man who expected to be obeyed*'.

> Morris never taught. One teacher concluded it was probably just as well because he '*was a bit awkward with children*'. But that mattered little, for following graduation he entered his chosen career - educational administration. It was the choice of many young men with similar views and background. Other Idealists notably Edward Holmes, Michael Sadler and Robert Morant led the way, all becoming influential administrators. Morris first secured the post of 'learner', or what we might currently label a 'graduate trainee', in Kent. E Salter-Davies Director of Education there seems to have specialised in selecting talented young men and coaching them in the rudiments of educational administration. However it is doubtful if he taught Morris much because before the year ended his new 'learner' applied for and attained the post of Assistant Secretary for Education in Cambridgeshire. References were provided by Salter-Davies; W E Johnson, his Cambridge tutor; Arthur Richmond, the Assistant Director at Kent, who had worked closely with Edward Holmes and Robert Morant at the Board of Education; and Hastings Rashdall. The latter assured the panel the applicant was '*a man of decided ability and great independence of thought and character ... who may be trusted to turn himself with abundant zeal and conscientiousness to whatever work he undertakes*'. Unlike many references penned on behalf of ex-students this was an honest and prophetic one. Sadly Rashdall died shortly after writing the reference, thereby never experiencing the satisfaction of witnessing the extent to which his student translated his ideals and hopes into reality.

Chapter Two

The plight of rural education

Morris was surely overjoyed to return to his beloved Cambridge. Renting rooms in Trinity Street he commenced the congenial lifestyle of dinner parties, vigorous weekend walks and long conversations on matters cultural, political and educational with friends which occupied his leisure time. As the wife of one ex-colleague explained in those years he lived surrounded by '*a circle of interesting and interested persons. Enjoying a very wide life*'. Conversations may not be the most apposite term, for according to a friend the Sunday walk was '*usually an occasion for a monologue by Henry as he declaimed and developed his ideas*' (Pritchard undated: 21). Appointed Assistant Secretary for Education to Austin Keen whom he described as '*insufferable, ignorant and intolerable*' (Ree 1973: 35) Morris became Secretary in 1922 when Keen unexpectedly died.

The comfortable, cultivated, cultured life of Cambridge dominated by the predictable cycle of the university calendar was diametrically at odds with the world beyond the City boundary. Cambridge was affluent; the County poor. Cambridge was awash with educational institutions (apart from the university there were primary, elementary, Grammar and numerous independent and private schools); the County was not. There most young people had access only to all age schools so even if they stayed beyond the minimum leaving age of twelve it rarely served any useful purpose. Without accessible higher grade schools the majority had little choice but to leave upon reaching

Standard IV, a level of attainment easily reached by the average ten-year-old.

The first two decades of the century saw the emergence of a plethora of radical and progressive schools (Woods 1920; Stewart 1972). Most reflected the predilections, not to say idiosyncrasies, of their founders but a common thread was a desire to unearth a middle way between on one side the muscular-Christianity of the public schools and state Grammar schools that aped them. And on the other the depressing rigidity of the Board or elementary schools. Although not mutually exclusive the progressive schools often fell into two categories. Some, like Bembridge founded by J H Whitehouse, placed great emphasis upon developing an affection for arts and crafts; others, such as Rendcomb, the Little Commonwealth established by Homer Lane in 1913, and Beacon Hill founded by Dora and Bertrand Russell in 1927, focused on the arts of self-governance stressing the importance of stimulating independence of thought. Morris was closer to the former. Apart from Teddy O'Neill (see Shute 1998) and Morris most of the leading figures in the world of progressive education operated outside the state system. Their common meeting ground however were the conferences and publications of the New Ideals in Education group.

During the 1920s one Cambridge school in particular attracted national and international attention - The Maltings funded by Geoffrey Pyke and administered by Susan Isaacs. Replicating the principles of the Laboratory School Chicago established in 1896 by Dewey, it opened in 1924. Following the departure of Isaacs it closed in 1929. In those brief five years it managed to achieve an influence '*out of all proportion to its lifespan or size*' (Stewart 1972: 261). Whether Morris met Isaacs or Pyke is not known, although it seems most likely their paths crossed in such a small City. Irrespective of physical contact he would have heard a great deal about this school endeavouring to create

> *an embryonic community life, active with types of occupations that reflect the life of the larger society, and*

permeated throughout with the spirit of art, history and science. (Dewey 1899: 43-4)

One would love to know what Morris made of Pyke, Isaacs and their experiment, sadly we will never find out.

The problems

Cambridgeshire as an education authority had no jurisdiction over the City. The relatively wealthy often well-heeled citizens of the latter looked after their own thereby avoiding the need to pay for the deprived rural hinterland encircling them. During the inter-war years Cambridgeshire was the second poorest County in England. Only Herefordshire raised a lower income from the imposition of a penny rate. The gap between the product of a penny rate in an urban and rural authority then far exceeded any differences between 'rich' and poor rural authorities.

Rural de-population, often viewed as a natural by-product of industrialisation, had by the 1920s been a feature British life for eighty years. Worcestershire in 1861 was the first to record an absolute decline in population but within a decade Cambridgeshire followed suit (Saville 1957: 55). Rapid population growth guaranteed the plight of young people in the fast expanding, socially unstable urban areas disproportionately attracted the attention and concerns of reformers and politicians. Those growing up in the tranquil countryside found their needs largely set aside. Year on year the gap in standards between urban and rural provision became more pronounced. Dwindling rolls and a deteriorating funding base prompted ever more school closures; lower capital investment in new school buildings; and a mounting backlog of repairs and desperately needed improvements. Closures ensured more pupils each year travelled further, frequently on foot, to attend school. Where closure was avoided it was often because other mechanisms were exploited to 'balance the books'. Examples included retention of all-age single teacher schools; employment of unqualified teachers; and paying qualified and unqualified alike substantially less than metropolitan colleagues.

Certificated women heads, for example, in rural schools during the inter-war period were paid on average half that of London colleagues (Hurt 1979).

It was assumed poor educational provision, the cultural vacuity of rural life and the historic lot of the farm worker '*poverty, dependence and remorseless labour*' (Newby 1980: 122) encouraged the best and most talented to desert the countryside. As Morris explained

> *Educationally the countryside is subordinate to the towns and its schools are dominated by, and are subservient to, the urban system of secondary and higher education. Owing to the operation of the free-place scholarships system, the abler children are taken from the country schools into the town secondary schools, where they receive a predominately literary and academic education under urban conditions divorced from the life and habits of the countryside. Either they are lost to the villages and become town workers, or return to their homes unfitted and untrained for life as countrymen and countrywomen. If, as seems possible, the number of urban secondary schools is increased, and the proportion of free places is universally raised from 25 to 40 per cent, the plight of the countryside will be intensified. Already many Education Authorities, confronted with the demand for increased secondary education, are considering schemes for additional secondary and central schools in the town to which country children are to be conveyed on a large scale by train and fleets of motor omnibuses.* (1924: 1)

Scholarships undoubtedly encouraged many of the 'brightest and the best' to leave but better paid and more secure employment, superior housing and the 'bright lights' also played their part. According to the Social Darwinists, who dominated official educational thinking during the inter-war years, selective migration of the 'better stock' to urban districts showed no signs of abating. Official statistics claimed to provide 'hard evidence' this was having a damaging impact. These showed double the incidence of mental defects amongst rural compared to urban children despite the benefits of a supposed healthier environment. Duncan along with other experts predicted the situation was worsening with the continual '*inter-marriage of inferior stock*' (1938: 18). Such an analysis confirmed, for some, the folly of disproportionately investing in the fabric of rural schools or employing qualified teachers if unqualified were available.

Morris encountered these problems and 'solutions' in abundance. First he inherited possibly the worst qualified teaching force in Britain. 49 per cent (national average 22 per cent) were uncertificated holding only a school-leaving certificate. A further 8 per cent were supplementary teachers, merely 'vaccinated and eighteen' lacking even a school-leaving certificate (Wise 1931). Second most schools were small, scattered, isolated and poorly housed. The County had 33 schools with an average attendance of less than 30, 14 with between 30 and 40 on roll, 12 between 50 and 60, and 41 with 60 to 100. This compared with only 21 between 100 and 250. In the small schools all 3 to 14 year olds were taught in a single room, except where numbers or space allowed for a separate infant class. Where that occurred, the Standard I to IV pupils were generally lumped together. Three-quarters of the all-age units in 1922 were Church of England maintained schools.

In 1930 Leonard and Dorothy Elmhirst, who provided financial and moral support for Morris, funded research by Marjorie Wise into the condition of rural schools. She visited schools across the country including Cambridgeshire. Wise tells of appalling neglect and low standards regarding teaching and buildings alike. Her research describes schools '*smelling of damp and boots*', with wet clothing being dried around a solitary stove that under '*normal conditions ... is barely sufficient to keep the room warm*'; of rooms so cold in winter '*the ice on the aquarium did not melt for five days*'; of '*high and ugly rooms ... with little in them that is beautiful*'; of schools without cupboards where desks and corners are '*piled up with books and materials*'; of a classroom '*twelve feet square and twenty feet high ... like a lift shaft - No sun! No room to run about! Bad ventilation*'; of thirty-six girls using pail toilets emptied once a month; and dirt and decay in profusion.

Examples of good buildings are quoted but Wise concludes '*to say that ten per cent*' fall within that category '*would be to exaggerate*' (1931: 27).

De-population alone cannot account for variations between urban and rural provision. The neo-feudal structure of rural society contributed a great deal to both the departure of the 'brightest and the best' and the failings of the school system. Financial domination by squirearchy and spiritual domination by clergy over many centuries manufactured across large swathes of the countryside a cowed population. Less money was spent on rural services in part because the squirearchy and middle-classes who controlled local government were loathed to sanction a rate adequate to pay for decent schools and services. Miserliness was only a partial explanation. Frequently councillors, or those who pulled their strings, were profoundly antipathetic towards public education. Some valued learning and willingly paid to privately educate their offspring but others were stupid ignorant individuals who held learning and matters cultural in profound contempt. Both groups despite their differences agreed little was to be gained from providing more than the minimum schooling the law obliged for the children of labourers, tradesmen and servants. Indeed they often feared the measly amount offered might disrupt the existing balance of power within the sylvan community. After all had not the 1906 Department of Agriculture Report on rural de-population confirmed '*modern education promoted discontent with the monotony of country life*' thereby making a bad situation worse. Teachers were therefore encouraged to stick with the old methods and expected upon pain of dismissal as one ex-pupil of a village school explained to '*make sure us poor children were brought up to respect their betters*' (interview quoted Martin 1965: 98).

Morris with his new fangled ideas and contempt for those who believed '*they will preserve the village by resisting*' (1936: 49) educational reform was fated to skirmish with some powerful figures in the local political and social hierarchy. Amongst these some came to loathe him. Influential landowners and businessmen such as the Spicers and

Huddlestons with good cause feared where his plans would lead. They knew his goal of ensuring '*the responsibilities of leadership and the maintenance of liberal and humane traditions in our squireless villages*' should '*fall on a larger number of shoulders ... on the whole community*' (1924: 29) jeopardised their status and authority. As they began to oppose him Morris correctly categorised them and their kind as the enemy. Others like the wealthy Lord Fairhaven who tolerated Henry, invited him to dinner but were too selfish and mean to make a worthwhile contribution, he despised. Whilst those such as Councillor Mrs Mellish-Clarke (whom he dubbed Mrs Hellish Clarke) he endeavoured to fight to a standstill. Predominately, according to a colleague though, his way of handling the landowners, farmers, dons and wealthy '*who could and did make his life even more difficult was by being secretive*'.

Endemic poverty, unemployment, under-employment, de-population and poor schooling were not features of rural life unique to Britain. Throughout Europe and the United States reformers for some time actively sought solutions to these problems and by 1914 a substantial literature existed on ways to enhance rural education. International conferences and study tours took place to introduce policy makers to good practice elsewhere, whilst successful programmes attracted visitors from around the world. Two developments received greater attention than most, the Danish Folk High School and American Consolidation High School. Although dissimilar in many respects both contributed to the concept of the Village College, although Morris was obdurate in his refusal to bestow upon them any kudos whatsoever. Each offered a divergent approach to surmounting the deficiencies of rural education. I will briefly consider these initiatives which attracted far more international attention than the Village Colleges, yet to a large extent thanks to Morris and his followers remain overlooked in Britain.

The American Consolidated School

Dual use of premises is a longstanding feature of American schooling. In 1845 Henry Barnard published his **Report on**

the Conditions and Improvement of Public Schools in Rhode Island, possibly the earliest American manifesto advocating the community school. It outlines the responsibility of schools for improving community and individual living (Scanlon 1959: Decker 1972). Already by the 1850s public pressure had secured a legal right of access to school premises for political and social events in some areas (Punke 1951). Before the century ended the nomenclature community school was being applied to differentiate a 'new type' of school in rural localities where school boards provided land, extensions and facilities for community usage.

Accounts of the failings of American rural education differ little from those penned by British writers. In the former the preferred solution was the 'scientific' amalgamation of small, especially single teacher units, into Consolidated Schools equipped to offer a broad curriculum and as a report commissioned by the Department of Agriculture explained serve as centres '*for the fullest expression of the community life*'. Consolidation first emerged as a coherent policy in Massachusetts in 1869 where comprehensive state funding and planning differentiated it from the British policy of random closures dictated by falling numbers.

From the onset the carrot to persuade local communities to 'surrender' their school was the promise of a new Consolidated School serving as a social and cultural centre providing recreation, support and education for all. Like Village Colleges these were envisaged as being manifestly different from 'urban schools' which instead of fuelling dissatisfaction with the rural way of life would promote affection for it. Vogt held this was achievable only via a radical departure from traditional approaches. Sustaining communities meant establishing institutions which ceased preparing young people for competition and instead taught service to others and the value of '*social culture and community progress*' (1917: 268). Vogt proposed eroding the historic dependency on town and city by creating schools offering rural communities a range of services of the highest quality including:

- an educational and cultural base;
- an art centre and gallery, containing works of the highest quality housed in school buildings '*as attractive and artistic as possible*' (ibid: 272);
- a museum preserving the archives and history of the community;
- a home for the local library;
- a base for public health services;
- a community social centre;
- social facilities where matters of local and national political concern might be debated and discussed.

Consolidated schools were perceived as the flagships of a new order for American rural education. Foght describes a number including the Porter Community School (Missouri) opened in 1913 where he encountered a remarkable range of community and regular school provision such as

> *a vacation school, agricultural short courses, cadet work for rural leadership, and the maintenance of social and economic clubs, musical organizations, nature study clubs, etc. for the young people as well as for their parents.* (Foght 1918: 153)

In addition to classrooms and workshops it possessed a fully equipped kitchen for community rallies; a five acre demonstration farm; play apparatus available for use before and after lessons; a community library; and model orchard. Investment on this scale may have been exceptional but by 1920 the concept of the community school was well established encouraging a belief that rural '*problems*' *might best be tackled via the provision of community services through the democratized rural school*' (Evans 1921: 577). An opinion based on the evidence that schools in a number of localities had '*dovetailed the school program into the community program; it has made itself the dynamic center of the community's entire social and economic life*' (Eggleston and Bruere 1913: 18). Illinois in 1917 passed a law providing for the establishment of '*community high schools and centers*' (Hacker 1929: 44) and other states followed. A decade later Burr reports '*in parts of the United States a very rapid development in the extending of the community high school*' (1929: 260).

The Danish Folk High School

The first Danish Folk High School opened in 1844. They do not cater for those of compulsory school age and are residential in character. As Morris (1941) pointed out, in an article written to deflect the criticism then circulating that Village Colleges were a pale imitation of the Folk High School, these traits made glib comparisons inappropriate. Unfortunately the desire to puff-up his reputation fuelled an ill-judged broadside exhibiting a lack of intimacy with their history or achievements. The crux of his case, previously trailed in the Memorandum, was that Folk High Schools were fatally flawed. Being residential meant they were divorced from the world they sought to change, therefore it was pre-ordained they would degenerate into mere hostels

> *to which a minority may escape, at infrequent intervals, the squalor and frustration of the contemporary town, does not begin to deal with the cultural needs of modern communities.* (1941: 79)

Morris decreed those seeking an appropriate educational structure for the English countryside had 'absolutely' nothing to learn from Folk High Schools. He was partially correct in arguing they sought to ameliorate the failings of the Danish school system. But they were not, as Morris implied, institutions concocted to provide a last-ditch remedial programme teaching again what was ineptly taught in the first place. N F S Grundtvig, their founder and undisputed leader of the movement during his lifetime, certainly had minimal faith in traditional teaching methods. For that reason they were deliberately quarantined from the '*schools of death*' where adults:

> *torment the young with questions they cannot possibly answer out of their own experiences of life, and can only answer by repeating the words of others.* (Grundtvig in Davies 1944: 39)

Schools would accomplish nothing socially positive, Grundtvig insisted, until there existed a cadre of teachers with the skills and desire to reform them. Therefore a network of Folk High Schools was created in part to furnish just such a vanguard (Thaning 1972). That however was merely one of many aims.

Grundtvig commenced his work at a low point in the history of Denmark. Progress towards a democratic political structure had stalled; a prosperous rural economy was falling into penury with the influx of cheap American grain onto European markets; and finally military defeat and subsequent annexation of the province of Schleswig-Holstein by Germany encouraged widespread despondency and a belief that Denmark and Danish culture and language had little future. Adopting the slogan "Outward Loss, Inward Gain" Grundtvig acted, inaugurating a national movement which within fifty years, according to an impressive array of commentators, transformed the Danish peasantry into the most enlightened, prosperous and well-educated in the world and helped create a vibrant democracy and sense of cultural identity (Haggard 1911: Sadler 1926: Foght 1915). Yet the High Schools eschewed vocational training opting instead to disseminate '*enlightenment for life*', endeavouring to send every student back to their communities with

> *heightened enjoyment, a clearer view of human and social conditions, especially in his own country, and with a revived feeling of national and popular unity which will make him share all the great and good deeds*

> *which have been done up to the present day and will in future be done.* (Grundtvig quoted Rordam 1965: 11)

Attendance was voluntary and free. High Schools were founded upon a concept of 'popular education' which envisaged each as an autonomous unit unfettered by state control or regulation; public opinion or public authority. Autonomy produced, as Grundtvig anticipated, rich diversity. Within decades this tiny country had dozens of High Schools of varying size; some affiliated to religious or political groups others not; some serving a locality, others a given occupation, trade or cultural pursuit. Each ultimately surviving as a consequence of an ability to meet student needs. Yet united in a belief that a

> *flourishing of national life demands a free and fruitful interaction between the different generations and social classes of the nation, not only a historical fellowship between past, present and future, but also a social fellowship which transcends all class differences.* (Manniche 1939: 87-88)

It was a vision almost indistinguishable from that of the Idealists and founders of the settlement movement.

Grundtvig visited Britain three times. He admired the creativity industrialisation unleashed; the work of Robert Owen, whom he met; and enjoyed a lengthy stay at Trinity College (Cambridge) which propagated a deep and abiding faith in the inherent value of corporate college life. These visits also promulgated a profound sense of foreboding. Convincing him Denmark must avoid replicating the '*dismal*' society which transformed workers into '*mere accessories, mere appendices to machines*' (quoted Davies 1931: 34). The repercussions of the enclosures that annihilated the peasantry and drove small farmers to the verge of extinction horrified him. This decimation of rural life created, he told Danes, '*the inner sore in England, which one easily overlooks, dazzled by her outward splendour*' (op cit).

Grundvitg's '*schools for life*' had a dual purpose. First, they sought to '*awaken, nourish, and enlighten*' (Grundtvig quoted Davies 1931: 72). '"*Know thyself*" *is the right inscription above all human school-doors*' he argued therefore students must be supported in their search for a personal philosophy to guide them through life. They were to be offered a journey of self-discovery linked to a search for '*culture and enlightenment which is the affair of each individual and bears its reward in itself*' (op cit). In so far as High Schools had a curriculum it focused on nourishing a love of history and language, literature and song. Instruction was not the aim, for Grundtvig believed enlightenment was achieved through '*the living word*' encountered in '*the free, the powerful talk*' which gave birth to the '*the winged word*' able to awaken individuals and nations (quoted Koch 1952: 138).

Second, their aim was to help students equip themselves for civic society. Whereas mainstream schools educated individuals '*to be critics instead of creators*' (ibid: 75) breeding inertia and a foreboding that nothing can be changed. Folk High Schools by enabling individuals to consciously be at one with the community generated a '*spiritual sense of unity in multiplicity*' (Grundtvig quoted Davies 1931: 73). Thereby it was hoped stimulating democracy and social reform by preparing students to be active citizens within a free society. Accordingly a spirit of freedom must pervade staff-student relationships as a:

> *living education is only found where the ear is as free as the mouth, and where the teacher really strives to serve his hearers with all the vital power and enlightenment which may be found in him and develop itself in him under the relationship.* (Grundtvig quoted in Davies 1931: 91)

Only by granting teachers the utmost independence within a structure where students comprised a majority on the managing Council, would this happen. To minimise conflict; encourage discourse and dialogue; and allow democratic structures to thrive, staff and students had to be given every opportunity to form a close community. To achieve this, courses were of three months duration thereby allowing students to immerse themselves in the life of the institution.

The High School movement like the YMCA, the first national and international youth organisation (also inaugurated in 1844), and the settlements, embraced a federalist structure of autonomous self-governing units. One devised to thwart annexation by a religious group or the state. So firm was this commitment to independence, that closure was viewed at one point as being preferable to a funding structure which gave the state leverage over course content (Begtrup, Lund and Manniche 1936).

Why did Morris so contemptuously dismissed Folk High Schools? Obviously their achievements before 1941 cannot be accurately quantified but educational reformers unanimously judged Denmark as pre-eminent regarding the quantity and quality of post-school provision (Schairer 1937). Sadler, who regarding background and philosophy was close to Morris, who as a Board of Education advisor investigated the Folk High Schools, American School Social Centers and Consolidated High Schools confidently concluded the former '*worked a miracle of culture in the Danish countryside*' (1926: 9). Allowing agriculture to prosper without recourse to protectionism because a '*mobile, intelligent, heartily co-operative*' peasantry had been produced by the High Schools. Davies (1931: 31) notes how High School graduates waged a productive '*war*' on traditional teaching methods - rote learning and mechanical repetition. Establishing the first modern 'free school' at Ryslinge in 1850. Kold, the founder, held children's education to be fundamentally the concern of parents not the state. Accordingly, the 'free schools' were co-operatively administered by parents. When Morris penned his attack several hundred operated under a compact negotiated between Kold and the government in 1856. The latter agreeing to provide funding without interfering '*in any way with the instruction of the pupils*' (Begtrup, Lund and Manniche 1936: 106).

Given the High Schools and related initiatives achieved so much of what Morris desired, why the antagonism? The answer probably lies in the aspirations of Grundtvig and his followers. Like Morris they wished to reinvigorate and protect the rural economy and lifestyle whilst curtailing the ascendancy of 'urban ways' but they had a parallel goal, one he instinctively recoiled from. Grundtvig and his followers were pluralists and libertarians distrustful of all governments. Attracted to diversity on ideological and pragmatic grounds; they embarked on a 'Long March' to preserve the cultural and political sovereignty of Denmark from the threat posed by a rapacious neighbour. Accordingly like every successful guerrilla movement, educational or military, they eschewed centralised administration in favour of a cell structure better suited to withstanding infiltration by hostile agents. It was a structure that served them well during wartime German occupation. When more than anywhere else Denmark repudiated collaboration and anti-semitism not least because the High Schools had created an intellectual *'bulwark against Nazism and Fascism'* (Moller and Watson 1944: 5: Rordam 1965).

Morris never shared this ingrained fear of centralisation. Believing decision-making should, where feasible, be delegated to local authorities was about as far as he went along that route. Contemptuous of politicians he nevertheless constantly courted them. Forever the outsider yearning to be an insider, stalking Ministers and officials, hoping eventually they would be converted to his big idea - and then oblige others to implement it. An intellectual quick to despise those in authority without his 'learning', their rebuffs usually served to confirm his prejudices. Yet he never lost faith with the system. Right until the end yearning for them, the mediocre politicians and satraps he privately sneered at, to bestow upon him a bigger bauble than his meagre CBE. One is often reminded of an irascible District Officer consigned to some far flung outpost - overlooked, taken-for-granted, difficult to manage but always doggedly loyal to the Imperial Mission. Morris was incapable of sharing a cramped dormitory with his students like Kold. Or the Spartan diet of poor country folk so they would not feel intimidated or uncomfortable. Here was an administrator bent upon creating a better world in his own image, determined in the process not to relinquish his power. By inclination and training Morris was a centralizer. Aware the control of the squire and vicar was fast fading he was determined to fill the vacuum with people crafted in his own image. The Folk High Schools which enthused and excited Jeffersonian liberals from the United States like Lindemann and Foght held no appeal for Morris. Whatever the High Schools achievements their rampant pluralism and the sheer untidiness of the structure they spawned affronted Morris. Both the autocrat within and the professional strategist without made him by inclination a planner. Able without a blush to propose, '*the town and countryside must be planned so that they will provide a way of life (the new democratic way of life)*' (quoted van der Eyken and Turner 1969: 145).

Morris boasted the Village Colleges '*would surpass anything achieved elsewhere*' and specifically would be '*more comprehensive*' (1924: 20) than American Consolidated Rural Schools. No account is offered as to how this was to be achieved. He knew sufficient about the Folk High Schools to pen a critique, albeit a shoddy one. Similarly, he must have been well acquainted with the American Consolidation and community school programme; the Social Centre movement; the public advocacy by Dewey of the linking of school and community; and the innovative work of Mabel Carney, who established a community school similar in many respects to the Village College. All of these strove to extend the community role of the school. After all, pivotal figures involved in these developments were known and respected within the educational circles in which he moved. It is inconceivable that someone active in the Adult Education Group chaired by St John Parry, a member of the Ministry of Reconstruction Committee which produced the 1919 Report; who was an invited member of the All Souls group of hand picked Chief Education Officers, HMIs, academics and MPs founded by W G S Adams; who knew personally a wide-circle of progressive educationalists including the Elmhirsts, who actively sponsored projects to cultivate rural education; and who made three visits to the United States, one as a consultant to the American government, could have been unaware of community school developments taking place elsewhere. Yet he did nothing to encourage others here to learn from those developments only mentioning them, if at all, in disparaging terms. This approach certainly helped secure his parochial reputation as the progenitor of the community school and inventor of community education. Retrospectively it doesn't matter if Morris did or did not purloin the ideas of others, his achievements make the charges an irrelevance. What has been unfortunate is given his pivotal position the wilful failure to publicise the thinking and experiences of others undertaking similar work elsewhere contributed to narrowing of the debate and a closing down of options in Britain.

The threat from across the border

Nationally rural education was a mess and in Cambridgeshire probably more so than almost anywhere. Doing nothing, an attractive tactic for those hoping the countryside would remain unchanged, was a dangerous option. Close by in Norfolk there was a clear indication this was no longer a viable choice. Edwardian England experienced an unprecedented wave of school strikes. Most took place in industrial areas where traditions of trade union and political activism were more securely embedded. Yet as Humphries' (1981) wonderful history recounts rural areas were not spared. Brutal, humiliating punishments and widespread discontent with the mind-numbingly dull content of lessons produced walk-outs and strikes which, for a while, spread like wildfire. Most were short-lived as parents, teachers and school boards formed an unholy Trinity of self-interest to coral the young people back to school. One strike though was different.

In Burston, near Diss in Norfolk the children went on strike in 1914 not because their teachers were cane wielding tyrants or their lessons tiresome renditions of the National Code but for the opposite of reasons. Here first pupils, then parents went on strike to prevent the dismissal of their teachers Kitty and Tom Higdon. The reasons for their plight are difficult to isolate, but both attended chapel. This upset the parson who as chair of the school managers expected his teachers to attend his church. Tom was also a part-time organiser for the Agricultural Labourers' Union and this offended the local farmers. Both were active in the Labour Party in the constituency - which was to return the first Labour MP elected for a rural seat; and Kitty was a unconventional teacher a '*very gentle woman ... a Christian Socialist ... a pacifist. I never knew her to cane or even slap a child*' (interview with Burston pupil Edwards 1974: 150). On the morning following their dismissal sixty-six children out of seventy-two went on strike in support of their teachers. It proved to be the longest strike in British history lasting from 1914 to 1939. At first the children had lessons on the village green, then in a carpenter's shop and eventually public subscription raised sufficient to build a new 'strike school'. It was opened before a crowd of 1,200 by seventeen year old Violet Potter one of the strike leaders with the words '*With joy and thankfulness, I declare this school open to be forever a school of freedom*' (Ward 1990: 158). Besides the front door an engraved stone boldly proclaimed

> THIS BUILDING WAS ERECTED BY PUBLIC SUBSCRIPTION TO PROTEST AGAINST THE ACTION OF THE EDUCATION AUTHORITIES TO PROVIDE A FREE SCHOOL TO BE A CENTRE OF RURAL DEMOCRACY AND A MEMORIAL OF THE VILLAGERS' FIGHT FOR FREEDOM

Symbolically Burston closed, owing the age and infirmity of Kitty Higdon, within weeks of Impington Village College opening. The Strike School throughout its existence posed a threat to the established order within the East Anglia and throughout rural England. Symbolising an alternative independent way forward which roundly rejected the old order and ways. Compared to Burston the Village Colleges must have seemed to the local councillors and landowners across the border a congenial alternative; compared to the Higdons Henry Morris an absolute Godsend.

Chapter Three

Buildings and visions

Henry Morris became Cambridgeshire's Chief Education Officer in 1922; he was 33. Russell Scott his Deputy, who briefly occupied the 'learner' post in Kent vacated by Morris, was 24. Between them they flaunted six years experience. Undeterred by youth or inexperience Morris embarked post-haste on implementing the most ambitious plan for reforming rural education ever attempted in Britain. Employing skills undoubtedly learnt whilst serving with the RASC Morris set to. Root and branch reform was he judged essential. For de-population and decline to be halted then reversed vibrant communities capable of retaining their 'brightest and best' were required. Superior schools and teachers would not suffice radically new institutions and educators were needed. Two potential impediments - the Church and the teaching profession - had initially to be either vanquished or converted if these were to be conjured up. Morris tackled the Church first.

With a third of all-age schools Church of England controlled, senior clergy had to be convinced reform posed no substantive threat to their interests. Otherwise it would be impossible to close the worst and coax the remainder into releasing their post-11 pupils to institutions providing secondary education. To achieve this Morris proposed introducing an Agreed Syllabus of Religious Instruction for all County schools acceptable to all denominations. This was easier said than done because within living memory all previous attempts to formulate such a syllabus had floundered amid acrimonious controversy. Applying prodigious guile Morris approached the Vice-Chancellor of Cambridge University The Reverend E C Pearce, a serving member Cambridgeshire Education Committee to chair a committee to compose a syllabus. Besides Pearce, and Morris as secretary, the Committee comprised fifteen of the 'great and the good' representing the principal Anglican and Non-conformist traditions. It proved a master-stroke, the committee produced an Agreed Syllabus by late 1923 acceptable to all parties. Nationally it was acclaimed as a breakthrough capable of ending the bickering between religious groups that was inhibiting the development of universal secondary education and consequently the separation of senior and junior education subsequently recommended by the Hadow Report in 1926. Acceptance of the Agreed Syllabus delighted local politicians because amalgamation created an opportunity for substantial savings, which proved helpful in winning over the teachers. This was achieved by persuading the Council to become possibly the first rural Education Authority to abide by nationally negotiated 'Burnham' rates of pay. Apparently at his first meeting with teachers following publication of the Memorandum his arrival was greeted by sustained applause. The stage was now set for the next step.

The Memorandum

During the summer of 1924 Morris stayed with J W Robertson Scott at Idbury Manor, near Kingham, Oxfordshire. There he prepared a Memorandum for submission to the Council. Robertson Scott was founder and editor of the monthly **The Countryman**. A radical campaigning journalist, previously a close colleague of W T Stead and H J Massingham, who authored over a dozen books on the 'rural problem'. Robertson Scott had a rural background but never farmed. A close friend of George Edwards (founder of the National Union of Agricultural Workers, the first Labour M P elected for a rural constituency, and supporter of the Burston school strike); a vocal Labour supporter; opponent of blood sports; a tee-totaller; and a sharp critic of the Established Church, in particular, and religion in general, Robertson Scott, like Morris, was '*an outsider in the countryside*' (Bonham-Carter 1971: 77). Scathing in his condemnation of the prevailing standards in rural schools he described them as '*ill-managed, ill-found, ill-taught*' (1925: 116). Morris returned from Oxfordshire with a manuscript which Cambridge University Press published privately. First copies were distributed to all members of the County Council over Christmas. They were sufficiently impressed to unanimously agree at the February 1925 council meeting to implement the Memorandum, but with the proviso that it must entail no additional expenditure.

The Memorandum still reads well. Compared to the turgid managerialist banality of most contemporary documentation emanating from schools, LEAs and government bodies it is a masterpiece of erudition. It still exudes an exhilaratingly radical edge, a sense of history and a vision of what might be. It reflects Morris's Idealist belief in the value of education and commitment to the notion that '*the ideal order and the actual order can ultimately be made one*' (Morris 1925: 11). Here is a statement of intent and guide to action. Writing about the Memorandum beguiles one into a desire to reproduce the original, what to omit becomes the challenge not what to incorporate. Certainly no précis can do justice to the language or appropriate the passion, excitement and breadth of the original. [It should be noted that two editions of the Memorandum are available. The first is the 1924 version prepared for the Council. A second revised edition was published in 1925 at the author's own expense by the Cambridge University Press.]

For Morris the goal was the creation of educational institutions distinctively different but equal to the best encountered in towns and cities. Institutions capable of furnishing the 'social and recreational life' country dwellers deserved. Achieving this he argued necessitated more

> *than the reorganisation of the elementary school system. There must in natural geographical centres be a grouping and co-ordination of all educational and social agencies... which now exist in isolation in the countryside.* (ibid: 4)

Unification and co-ordination were essential not solely to eradicate duplication and accomplish economies of scale, although Morris believed these would result, but primarily to ensure the institutions were large enough to marshal the resources required to enhance rural life, and to facilitate a reconstruction of rural education. Blessed with the resources needed to secure '*the development and enrichment of the curriculum, and ... training of teachers*' (ibid: 3).

Perhaps the best account of what he was hoping to achieve at this time appears in an article published in the house journal of progressive educationalists **New Ideals Quarterly.** It could still serve as a manifesto for community education and the community school movement:

> *At the present moment our state system of education is concerned almost wholly with children and the teachers of children. We ought to see our way to the organic provision of education for the adult community. We must do away with the isolated school. We must so organise the educational buildings of the towns and countryside that the schools of the young are either organically related to, or form part of, the institutions in which the ultimate goals of education are realised. We must associate with education all those activities which go to make a full life - art, literature, music, festivals, local government, politics. This is as important for the teaching of the young, as it is for the teachers themselves ... It is only in a world where education is confined to infants and adolescents that the teacher is inclined to become a pundit or tyrant.*
>
> *We should picture a town or village clustering around its educational buildings, with its hall, library, and recreation grounds, where young and old not only acquire knowledge but are inducted into a way of life.... We should abolish the barriers which separate education from all those activities which make for adult living... it should be the first duty of education to concern itself with the ultimate goals of education... Man's life as an economic, social and religious animal - that is the subject matter of education and education the means*

whereby he achieves the best in all respects... It is the life the adult will lead, the working philosophy by which he will live, the politics of the community which he will serve in his maturity that should be the main concern of education. (1926: 4-5)

The Plan

Morris was convinced the needs of the countryside would not be met until the rural elementary school system was '*recast*' and villages given primary and secondary education capable of '*fitting*' their young people for life '*in its widest sense*'. The schooling had to lead somewhere, therefore higher and technical education reflecting the needs of rural society must be readily accessible. To prosper these must be located within communities possessing a '*social and recreational life based on stable foundations*' (1925: 2). Pale imitations of the urban model were not required. Morris was convinced the first essential for establishing a rural civilisation with '*chronic vigour*' was the creation of '*a localised and indigenous system of education in its own right*' (ibid: 2).

Providing elementary, technical and higher education as well as stable and vigorous communities within the countryside Morris argued required more than reorganisation of the school system, it demanded '*a new institution, single but many-sided*' (ibid: 4). This new institution was the Village College. The Memorandum envisaged ten as sufficient to provide a foundation for a network that would eventually serve the whole County. Each would incorporate:

- A primary school for those aged 5 to 10 living in the village where it was located;

- A secondary school catering for 250 to 400 11 to 15 year olds drawn from a cluster of villages. This would possess specialist rooms and laboratories suitable for day and evening class use;

- An auditorium for assemblies, mid-day meals, physical education, plays, concerts, film shows, social events, public meetings and lectures;
- A library and public reading room for school students and community;
- A specialist room for agricultural education;
- Common and lecture rooms for adult education, village meetings and use by affiliated societies and clubs;
- Shower baths and changing rooms for school students and sports clubs;
- Sport and recreation grounds for the use of all;
- An infant welfare centre;
- Land for a school garden;
- Rooms and facilities for indoor recreation such as billiards;
- Houses on site for the Warden, up to five teaching staff and caretaker;

- Teaching staff of a new ilk '*country-bred*' and university educated '*with a love of and understanding of rural life with powers of leadership*' (ibid: 9).

At a time when rural education was an absolute mess; an economic slump was developing apace; and demographic trends pointed to a fall nationally of almost a third in the demand for school places between 1920 and 1940 plans to build on this scale were highly ambitious. Few contemporaries, one suspects, could have imagined Morris would even partially meet his target.

Getting the colleges built

Morris, like others, mistakenly assumed the expansionist 1918 and 1921 Education Acts would activate an enormous increase in educational building, similar to that generated by the earlier 1870 Act. This time Henry pleaded the opportunity to create a new architecture should not be surrendered through '*dullness and lack of courage*' for here was a unique chance to construct buildings capable of touching

> *every side of the life of the inhabitants of the district in which it is placed ... A building that will express the spirit of the English countryside which it is intended to grace, something of its humaneness and modesty, something of the age-long and permanent dignity of husbandry; a building that will give the countryside a centre of reference arousing the affection and loyalty of the country child and country people, and conferring significance on their way of life? If this can be done simply and effectively, and the varying needs which the village college will serve realised as an entity and epitomised in a building, a standard may be set and a great tradition may be begun; in such a synthesis architecture will find a fresh and widespread means of expression. If the village college is a true and workable conception, the institution will, with various modifications, speed over rural England; and in course of time a new series of worthy public buildings will stand side by side with the parish churches of the countryside.* (Morris 1924: 10-11)

The slump duly materialised producing in its wake harsh cut-backs in central and local government expenditure. By 1925 Morris knew the Village College network would become another educational pipe-dream unless hitherto untapped funding was unearthed. How the four colleges opened before the Second World War were funded is a fascinating story recounted by a number of writers (Ree 1973; Farnell 1968; Dybeck 1981). Basically cash was procured by consolidation (the closing of small uneconomic schools) and Morris himself. Holidays and spare time were devoted to cajoling potential benefactors and charitable trusts into giving donations. For example in 1929 Morris borrowed his fare to the United States to beg a grant from the Spelman Foundation. Sawston the first Village College completed in 1930 was typically paid for via a combination of gifts of land and labour, grants and bequests. The Carnegie Trust gave £5,500 for the 'village hall' element; the villagers raised £500; the site was donated by Spicers the local paper-makers; Mr and Mrs Spicer each donated £500; Leonard and Dorothy Elmhirst of Dartington Hall sent £1,000 to furnish a metal workshop; the Electricity Company wired the College without charge; Cambridge University Press presented books to the value of £100; and Newnham College provided the laboratory benches. A normal school of similar size would have cost £6,000 which gives some indication of the enormous extra effort involved in funding the Colleges. Costs on this scale meant however, as Dybeck points out, the Village Colleges '*only got off the ground because of the generosity of individuals and non-governmental bodies and not through any collective desire of the people*' (1981: 57).

Funding may have been cobbled together but Morris rarely cut corners because, according to a friend, '*his sharp eye for beauty and his hatred of the second best were his most profound characteristics*' (Fenn undated: 17). The Colleges deserved only the best so even their launch had to be special. Morris viewed the inauguration of Sawston as such a momentous event that it must be performed by royalty. So Edward, Prince of Wales, who initially assumed it was to be the opening of a university college and was most miffed to discover it was 'only a school' grudgingly did the honours.

Sawston today seems a somewhat lacklustre edifice. Lacking the cache of Impington designed by Walter Gropius and Maxwell Fry and described by Nicholas Pesvener as '*One of the best building of its date in England, if not the best*' (1954: 318); and denied the splendid setting of Linton; it was nevertheless, as Ree reminds us, by the standards prevailing in 1930 'revolutionary'. After all here was the first state school to have a separate hall; an appropriately furnished adult wing; a library for school and community use; a medical services room; playing fields with changing facilities for pupils and community; plus a Warden's house. This was at a time when the still current 1914 school building regulations suggested inside toilets for pupils were undesirable on health grounds. Fortunately by some miracle the health of civil servants, Members of Parliament, customers of the Ritz Hotel and the royal family apparently were not jeopardised by such an expensive novelty.

Attention to design and the provision of facilities however opulent were only part of the agenda. After all Morris was not merely devising a better class of school, a well-furnished version of the '*isolated elementary school, ... with all the narrower conceptions associated with it*' (Morris 1925: 5). Therefore securing a balance between the constituent elements was crucial if it was to be a community, cultural and educational centre. The school could not be allowed to eclipse the other crucial elements either with respect to access to the building or staff time. Within the Memorandum this balance and harmony was illustrated with one wing representing adult activities, another the school and bridging them the social and welfare provision for the whole community:

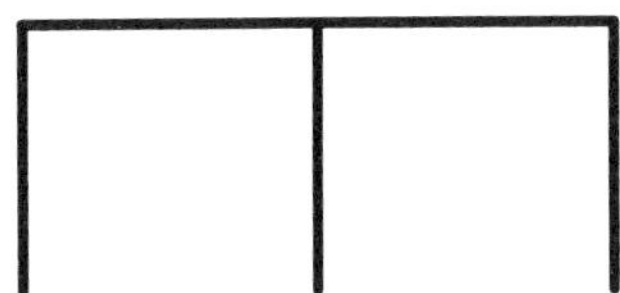

Achieving this equilibrium meant ensuring teachers were not allowed to revert to type, succumbing to the temptation to become a '*pundit or a tyrant*'. Once that happened the welfare, social and cultural roles would be marginalised and left to others. Therefore Morris needed to address three key aspects - how to create a curriculum coinciding with his aspirations; how to ensure internal equilibrium to prevent domination by one element of the equation; and finally how to secure sympathetic staff.

Search for a curriculum

Regarding the curriculum the challenge was how to concoct and deliver one which fostered within the school students a life-long affiliation and '*an affection for their school and their schooling*' (Burton 1944: 70); one germane to their lives and environment, yet avoiding narrow vocationalism. Also it must offer staff the prospect of creatively expressing their own personality and academic and intellectual preoccupations rather than delivering the old gruel in new bowls. Luck at least was on his side with regards this challenge. For in 1926 the government abandoned the National Code their equally sterile version of our National Curriculum. Matriculation, the pre-requisite for entry into a university or professional training, gave Grammar schools little flexibility regarding timetable and curricula content but non-selective schools, such as the Village Colleges, discovered abandonment of the Code bestowed on them an unparalleled freedom to forge new curricula. This autonomy survived until the mid-1950s, when, piecemeal, they began to encourage students to enter for external examinations. In Cambridgeshire Impington in 1953 became the first to create a 'Grammar School' stream. Theoretically this discontinued the need for those who passed the Eleven-Plus to travel to Cambridge to follow examination courses. Simultaneously it allowed 'late developing' Eleven-Plus failures to join the examination stream and take 'O' and 'A' Levels. Henceforth the Village Colleges could provide for 'all' the young people within the community, although invariably some parents still opted for a 'real' Grammar and independent education elsewhere. To avoid replicating the selective tripartite system within a single building it became necessary to impose a modified Grammar school curriculum to facilitate transference between 'streams'. Thus gradually ended a sojourn lasting approximately three decades during which Colleges were free to create a curriculum '*conterminous with life*' (Morris 1926: 38). Released from the burden of the Code, and as yet unencumbered with the yoke of external examinations or the current Code introduced by 1988 Education Act, Village Colleges to varying degrees seized this unique opportunity for experimentation, to '*become centres of corporate life and not congeries of classrooms for discourse and instruction*' (Morris 1926: 39).

Morris energetically bolstered those seeking to create a curriculum embracing the '*practical, aesthetic and intellectual*' (Burton 1944: 69). Not least by encouraging a movement away from didactic methods to those which give a '*place to conversation*' (quoted Ree 1973: 25), enabling teachers and scholars to engage in '*real work together*' so they '*would launch at once into creative service*' (op cit). The recruitment of Nan Youngman, with her links to Marion Richardson and the Arts and Craft Movement, as Art Adviser in 1944 reflected this ambition. It was as Stewart Mason (Jones 1988) noted as inspirational an act in its way as the engagement of Gropius. For Youngman shared with Morris a conviction that art had a vitally important role to play in the school setting. Determined to remove the pallid reproductions dotted around the schools she initiated a scheme whereby the authority purchased works by living artists for loan to the schools. She also organised study weekends and in-service training programme designed to transform the primary schools. The results were remarkable, as Mason an HMI covering the Cambridgeshire area during this period divulged, what he encountered there provided a model and vision of '*what an ideal primary school might be like*' (Jones 1988:29).

The flaw in viewing Morris as either the sponsor of great school architecture or curriculum reformer is that it risks overlooking the symmetry between the two. The Colleges may be beautiful, certainly daring but they were never intended to be purely decorative. Others planned, even erected, community schools which contrived to deliver a similar range of services, but probably only Robert Owen, before or since, with similar clarity grasped the necessity for creating new architectural forms capable of complementing and stimulating curricula reform. Owen and Morris comprehended the futility of striving to graft onto the traditional school, to inject into the boxed classroom, educational forms they are neither designed nor intended to accommodate. His appreciation of this dynamic rightly earned Morris the enigmatic title bestowed on him by Farnell of 'Architect of Education'.

Achieving a balance

The second challenge was to achieve a balance between the various activities and roles of the Village College. Two approaches were adopted. One was to restrict the size of the school population. Self-evidently the fewer school students the easier it would be to prevent the other components of college life being swamped and the energies of the Warden disproportionately consumed by the task of managing the school element. The first six colleges had planned intakes ranging from 218 (Bottisham) to 372 (Arthur Mellows, Glinton). Manageable numbers and an absence of pressure derived from externally imposed curricula allowed the Warden and staff to engage in a wide range of community activities. Granting the former time and freedom to organise health promotion programmes; supervise the payment of unemployment benefit; establish and support local voluntary groups; manage the delivery of a gamut of College based local authority services; and perform the expected social and community education roles. As a result like missionaries they ventured out into the villages and hamlets, attending meetings and visiting homes explaining what the Colleges had to offer, spreading the gospel of education.

The other ploy was to carefully design the buildings to promote integration and equilibrium. Impington, amongst the pre-war Colleges, perhaps most emphatically reflected this goal. A beautiful building without boundary walls to keep the community out or the students encased within, it is approached via a short drive past a great chestnut tree that commands the front lawn. The facade is dominated by the Hall that stands above the entrance with the Adult Wing sweeping away on one side and the classrooms on the other. Once inside one encounters a great concourse and, everywhere, natural light filling rooms and corridors. Nothing is cramped and wherever feasible classrooms look out upon countryside and open space. It remains to this day a superlative example of public architecture. Two researchers surveying community centres visited Impington shortly after it opened. After remarking on a failure to provide storage space for chairs and an uncomfortable draught from the front entrance they enthused:

> *the most excellent thing about the College is that the three major parts of the building have been very skilfully planned in their relation to one another. The classroom wing, the adult wing, and the Assembly Hall are situated so that their functions can be fulfilled quite independently ... they are knit together into a unified whole.* (Stephenson and Stephenson 1942: 33)

The wings were of approximately equal size. During a school day pupils and community shared corridors, toilets, entrances and hall but in other respects were confined to their respective wings. At other times the building became one.

Classrooms were designed to a standard then more usually encountered in a university than a school; as a consequence they were wholly appropriate for adult classes and meetings. So exceptional was the calibre of the building and fitments, pictures of the Colleges were regularly employed to exemplify what planners and administrators should aspire to. For example, Hardie (1947) employs an exterior shot of Impington to convey what County Colleges would be like; Dent (1946) a photo of the same College to depict secondary modern classrooms of the future; Sharp (1940) a view of Linton Village College to portray how school buildings might enhance rather than impoverish a rural landscape; Stillman and Cleary (1949) show Linton library, Bottisham and Impington classrooms, and the grounds of Impington to epitomise the finest school architecture. The latter even draw the readers attention to the exceptional quality of the classroom furniture. Morris devoted prodigious amounts of time to matters of design whether it be the most appropriate wood for hall panelling, the style of the classroom chairs or the flowers and shrubs for gardens and borders. This behaviour reflected not an overbearing and fussy personality but a determination to create a new type of educational institution, closer in terms of appearance and ambience to a university college or settlement. An unshakeable belief that people deserved only the best and that it was the duty of educators to give it to them. His Colleges were not, if he could prevent it, ever going to be allowed to degenerate into anything approximating to a traditional school. Such an intention was clearly signalled by the decision to call them colleges not schools; and have them administered by Wardens, like a university college or settlement, not head teachers. It was symptomatic of this approach that he described Impington not as a school but as '*the most advanced rural community centre in this country*' (quoted Ree 1984: 7), whilst the College brochure informed visitors it was '*A Community Centre housing a Secondary Modern School*' (Rowntree and Laver 1951: 325). The BBC North American Service in 1942 invited Morris talk on the Village Colleges. During the broadcast he described both his own philosophy and Impington, as follows:

> *For twenty years, I have been working at my job as an educationalist fired by the belief that the school in England, indeed in every country in the world, has to be remade; and I know that millions of ordinary men and women in all countries, looking back on their childhood, think the same. What has been wrong and what is still largely wrong? First of all the object of the school everywhere has been dominated by the exceptional needs of the "brainy" boy or girl who is good at books and comes out well in written examinations and who wins the prizes at the universities. Now these boys and girls are a minority in every country, though a precious minority - in England they are between five and ten per cent of all boys and girls in schools. Even for them this academic education is not wide enough. And for the millions of boys and girls who learn by practice and action it is a gigantic error. Secondly, the characteristic fallacy of adolescent education everywhere in the world is that teachers try to teach the boy and girl subjects and ideas which are more fitted for adult life - both in science, the arts and religion. Of course the education ought to be given in terms of the experience and*

instincts of adolescence. Thirdly, the main instrument of education in the School everywhere has been discourse by word of mouth and based on books. Schools have been classroom-ridden, textbook-ridden, information-ridden.

How is all this to be corrected? The answer is slowly taking shape in many countries. In England, which I know best, the Senior School is showing the way in town and country. What is the secret of the Senior School seen at something like its best? I cannot do better than take you to a country school a few miles from the University Town of Cambridge - the Village College of Impington, designed by the great architect Walter Gropius, now Professor of Architecture at Harvard University. The secret of the Senior School is activity - the major road to knowledge both for children and grown-ups. Here the dismal reign of mere chalk and talk, of the mechanical use of the textbook and the piling-up of parrot facts unrelated to the child's experience is finished. The school has become a society with a way of life. On any morning of the fateful summer you would see the boys and girls coming from ten villages on foot, on bicycle or bus, 350 of them full of zest. The morning assembly is a cheerful affair bright with music and hymns with the Bible lesson read by a pupil. Within a few minutes you would see the school becoming a hive of constructiveness. One group is in the six-acre garden with its adjacent laboratory and green house. Here all kinds of vegetables and fruit are grown for experiment and demonstration. Seeds and manures are tested, pigs, poultry and bees are cared for and fed, accounts and records are carefully kept, flower gardens and lawns are beautifully tended. It is a school estate in which the simplest boy in due course can acquire for life an understanding of a fundamental scientific law that affects all living experience - the law of cause and effect. Come to the wood and metal workshops. Here boys, and girls too, are making real things for the house and the garden, using what has been well called the "thinking hand". Thus they satisfy a manual instinct as old as the human race. Furthermore they learn the more surely how to measure, how to add, subtract and multiply, because all these mathematical operations are given meaning and reality. Again in the rooms for cookery and housewifery and infant welfare vital needs and instincts are the medium of training. Note another point of interest. It is that history and geography start from the history and geography of the surrounding countryside - from its industries, its agriculture, its geological formation, its rivers, its plant life, its beasts, birds, moths and butterflies. Impington Village College is a Community Centre of the Arts where children can consume and enjoy cooperatively all the art forms which otherwise would be impossible. One of the most interesting sights is a group of boys and girls doing rhythmic dancing under the leadership of Mr Kurt Joos, whose ballet is as famous in America as it is in Europe. Another is to hear music played or sung by orchestra and choir; another to see the dramatic act done sometimes to make more vivid a great point of history, or for the delight of the spoken word and the dramatic situation. Let me come to a favourite theme of mine. I always feel that the midday meal can be one of the most significant incidents in the life of the Senior School. The common meal has been one of the main instruments of education in civilization east and west. The common meal is not an extra at Impington. It has a place of honour in the curriculum. The tables are charmingly set out, there is a fine sung Grace, the children sit together with their teachers, there is an interval between the courses (a great artist said "slowness is beauty"), at the end there is music or a reading. Here is a scene of happiness, gaiety and health. A boy or girl who has sat through these common meals for four or five years will have acquired sound food habits for life and a fund of good manners. The Senior School can thus provide for the mind and the emotions, and for the play and exercise of body which youth demands. What of the spirit and religion? The Senior School at Impington tends to make even religion a thing of reality for the adolescent and that cannot be done by preaching and exhortation. The Senior School must be a society in which the growing boy and girl have hourly and daily opportunities of practising in a way they can understand what have been finely called the actions of religion., in particular cooperation, unselfishness, helpfulness, kindness, affection, trust. We fail miserably when we try to educate boys and girls under eighteen in the methods appropriate to men and women of twenty-one to thirty, and in no sphere is it truer than in religious education. I must close with a note at once both of counsel and of prophecy. The school is not enough. Indeed a good deal, perhaps a major part of what we have done in the school, may be lost unless we do something more. We begin to enter more fully into the world of reality at the age of sixteen, and the golden time for education, especially self-education, which is the most real form of education, is between the ages of sixteen and thirty. Every country in the world needs a fully developed system of adult education. Universal adult education is, I believe, the one way available by which humanity can begin effectively to solve its problems and to make civilization a success. In England and in America it is being realized that the school should be part of a community purpose and programme, both in the town and country. This is not an idle dream. In my own county of Cambridge all our Senior Schools are designed as part of a community centre serving a rural region. Impington, for instance, is designed so that all its workshops and laboratories can be used by both adults and adolescents, but apart from these there is special accommodation set apart for adults, lecture rooms, library, billiard rooms, committee rooms, common room and canteen. You may go there any evening and, though there is a war on, you will find some hundreds of young people and parents enjoying a general programme of lectures, crafts, games, dance, cinema or simply sitting in the common room over a cup of coffee and a magazine. The Senior School here is indeed not isolated but part of a community pattern. That blueprint is, I believe, valid for the countryside everywhere. Indeed, I hold that all town and country planning ought to have as its final object the cultural and recreational life of the adult community.

> *Such in brief is Impington. I said to one of the boys, "How do you like this?" "Oh, Sir," he replied, "It's fine. It's so much better than school!"*

The concluding anecdote is highly revealing and complements another oft recounted tale, both of which tell us a great deal about his mindset. Apparently Morris on one occasion was raging at a recalcitrant Warden regarding some misdemeanour until finally running out of invective he terminated the tirade with the accusation that the Warden's College was beginning to '*look like a bloody school*'.

His desire was always to bequeath future generations buildings that enhanced the environment and the lives of those coming into contact with them. An aesthete, never a utilitarian he believed, as he explained in a marvellous speech delivered to the Royal Institute of British Architects that;

> *The design, decoration and equipment of our places of education cannot be regarded as anything less than of first-rate importance - as equally important, indeed, as the teacher. There is no order of precedence - competent teachers and beautiful buildings are of equal importance and equally indispensable ... We shall not bring about any improvement in standards of taste by lectures and preachings; habitation is the golden method. Buildings that are well-designed and equipped and beautifully decorated will exercise their potent, but unspoken, influence on those who use them from day to day. This is true education. The school, the technical college, the community centre, which is not a work of architectural art is to that extent an educational failure.* (Morris 1945: 103 - 104)

Morris saw the buildings, landscape and public works of art we encounter in our daily round as powerful educators. Which mould and fashion us. Like Plato he perceived it to be the duty of the true educator to ensure these silent educators cumulatively act as subtle forces for good. That was why he pugnaciously sought the services of the best architects and demanded from those imposed on him by others the highest standards; why he and Jack Pritchard personally paid Walter Gropius and Maxwell Fry to design Impington. It explains his determination to fill the Colleges with works of art of the highest affordable quality. Content in the early days with quality prints he subsequently insisted the Colleges should display only original works of art, proclaiming on one visit that he'd *'rather see a dead cat on the wall than a reproduction'*.

Some who knew him suggest his greatest disappointment was the refusal of the County Council to purchase Henry Moore's 'The Family Group' to bestow on a College, after Moore offered it to Morris at a 'bargain' price. Moore is on record as saying it was as a result of his conversations with Morris about the thinking behind the Village Colleges he formulated his vision of a series of works on the family. Gallingly Morris had to stand aside whilst John Newsom, Hertfordshire's Director of Education, 'stole' the statue for a Stevenage school. It is said Morris never forgave Newsom even though Moore, by way of consolation, gave Henry a maquette of the statue.

Reviewing early accounts of Village College life one is frequently struck by the anonymity of the 'school' students. Depictions of College life by Rowntree and Lavers (1951), Baker (1953), Joad (1945) and, to a lesser extent, Dent (1943) tend to marginalise the 'day' school experience. Farnell (1968) however shows the 'school students' as enthusiastic advocates. Indicative of their affiliation is the extraordinarily high numbers attending evening classes and activities, over 70 per cent were under 18 (Baker 1953: 95). This compares to 45 per cent nationally (Sherman 1944: 57), a figure based on research showing rural localities consistently scoring below the average. Stephenson and Stephenson (1942: 30) confirmed that 14 to 18 year olds predominated amongst the students of formal evening classes at Impington. They also estimate over 10 per cent of the adults in the catchment area attended evening classes with far more involved in social and welfare activities. Levels of engagement might have been expected to decline as the novelty wore off but this did not occur. By 1954 Bracey (1959: 218) estimates over a quarter of the adults residing within the Impington catchment area were regular users. Up until the late 1960s the evidence points to Village Colleges achieving remarkable levels of association. Transcending the limitations of the 'dual-use' institution, to become something uniquely different - community, cultural and educational centres serving a broad spectrum of the local population. As Joad, a harsh critic of schools, argued the Village Colleges appeared to have uniquely broken

> *through the ring fence with which education is surrounded and to let the air of ordinary social life into the vacuum ... have transformed the conception of education. It is no longer a process which is abruptly truncated at fourteen; it continues throughout life.* (1945: 134)

If that was so then the aspirations of Morris had to a large extent been realised.

Staffing the colleges

Farnell suggests Morris was not generally '*a great admirer of school-teachers*' (1968: 80). Certainly he believed no professional group was '*more intellectually leaderless*' (Morris 1941: 72). This matched a disdain for the bulk of British education '*classroom-ridden, lesson-ridden, textbook-ridden, information ridden, and given over to incessant didactive discourse and discursiveness*' (Morris 1941: 69). So deficient, in his view, were the teacher training colleges that few emerging from them were in his opinion competent to meet the challenge of working in a Village College (1926: 37). Staff therefore were generally hand-picked, and if mistakes were made, as the Education Committee minutes indicate, ways were often found of removing those falling below the rigorous standards of intellect and commitment expected. Exceptional demands on their time have usually been the lot of rural teachers. Frequently others in the community anticipated they would immerse themselves in village life, shouldering heavy social and administrative burdens. The Village College programme extended and formalised those responsibilities. As Morris told one applicant for the post of Warden '*this is a 24 hour a day job*'. He wanted a servant to, and leader of, the community. A person who possessed the intellectual capacity to educate, not merely instruct. Someone with the stature to fill the vacuum of leadership within rural England stemming from a loss of religious faith and the demise of the old order. According to one Warden the resultant person-specification eventually incorporated the '*characteristics of Sir Galahad, Ignatius Loyola, Job and Machiavelli*' (Bowen 1973: 103). Plus, the wife of one ex-Warden explained, the DIY skills of a Barry Bucknell for in the early days Sunday was frequently devoted to mending fences, fixing guttering and tidying flower beds.

To compensate for the shortcomings of available staff a programme of in-service education was proposed. University and Village Colleges would be linked with the former delivering extra-mural courses designed to eradicate the cultural and intellectual isolation of rural teachers and surmount their wretched training. The Colleges were expected, much as the medieval universities described by Rashdall, to safeguard a threatened rural civilisation. Like Barnett's settlements Morris visualised the Colleges as communities serving the community. The model was never another school but the Oxbridge colleges, Grundtvig admired and Morris daily observed from his Cambridge flat; so it was naturally assumed a university don should sit on the governing body. Symbolic affiliation and a few extra-mural classes were helpful but the substantive involvement Morris yearned for eluded him. Myopic arrogance and wilful indifference within the university sector towards the educational needs of the community then, as now, ensured such integration never materialised. Only money, never an appeal to higher ideals, secures university patronage on the scale he required, and Morris had none to spare. He never secured the depth of collaboration the Land Grant System in the United States, which links community involvement to funding, has produced between state universities and community schools (Lerner 1996). Without university patronage creating a unique cadre of Village College staff elevated above the norm, alternative strategies were called for. Morris resorted to exhortation; painstaking, at times, inspired selection; and rigorous, even oppressive, supervision reinforced by surprise tours of inspection. Stewart Mason, who admired him immensely abhorred this latter practice, yet rationalised it on the grounds the Colleges

> *were his vision and his darlings and he interfered too much; he would keep on visiting them and get frightfully upset if he saw a bit of paper on the floor or dead flowers in a vase. All this interference in what, to him, were important matters, seemed petty and aggravating to the principal of a village college. Dudley Phillips, warden of Bottisham College, a very active man and also a visionary in his own way, used to be driven nearly mad with rage.* (interview in Jones 1988: 30)

Even allowing for hyperbole Wardens had exorbitant demands placed upon them. Like settlement Wardens they were expected to 'live in', thereby providing a bridge twixt 'community and College', 'town and gown'. Always accessible and purposefully located at the heart of the community they served. They were to co-ordinate, in the manner of a District Officer, delivery of the full diet of local services. Prior to the annexation of many welfare services by central government this entailed responsibility for the disbursement of unemployment benefit, co-ordinating local authority health care for mothers and children, plus oversight of provision such as the library or careers service which were integrated within the College.

Besides the support given by teachers, secretarial staff and volunteers the Warden stood alone. Then during the 1950s the appointment of first adult and subsequently youth tutors eased the load. The arrival of 'community staff' coincided with a rapid expansion in pupil numbers as a consequence of - the raising of the school-leaving age to 15; the sharp rise in the birth-rate between 1943 and 1950; and the decision of non-selective secondary schools to offer examination courses. Adult and youth tutors proved a mixed blessing. Indisputably they expedited an expansion in community provision on site and, often for the first time, in satellite villages. Their advent however signalled the onset of an ever more discernible division of labour twixt teaching and 'community staff'. Henceforth the former tended to detach themselves from voluntary community work, deemed the purview of the paid professional or part-timer; whilst the latter perceived themselves either as appendages of the Warden or school-based emissaries of a County Hall controlled community education service. Divergence became enshrined in the demarcation of responsibilities as Colleges expanded. Staff fragmented into departmental and managerial hierarchies created around a 'career structure'. This was built upon a taxonomy of special responsibility posts enshrined in a national pay structure which delineated the number of these allotted to each school according to intake. Wardens by the 1960s were located at the pinnacle of a managerial structure. Immediately below were a Deputy Head(s) with a specific remit for the day-to-day management of the 'school', then a plethora of departmental, pastoral and subject posts all acquiring their status by exaggerating the demarcation of responsibilities. Each and every pressure - the expansion of pupil numbers; fragmentation of the teaching profession; streaming; and emergence of specialist youth and community workers and adult educators, cumulatively militated against the survival of the integrated collegiate model Morris desired. Yet despite the advent of adult and youth tutors, as the following account indicates, incumbents retained into the 1970s a daunting roll-call of tasks: being

> *responsible for the full range of Village College activities. He is Head Master of the school, supervises all adult and youth organisation in the College, acts as area Careers Advisory Officer and has oversight of the branch of the County Library attached to the College. It is his responsibility to maintain that continuity of education which is at the heart of the Village College concept. As Head Master, he is in close touch with educational developments in the county and has the same duty as any other Head to the pupils in his care. He is not only responsible for the efficient*

> *administration of adult Further Education in the College but he must also closely involve himself with other cultural activities in the area and must see that the College is ready to assist in their development in every possible way. He must see that the life of the community is enriched by lectures, recitals, demonstrations of skill, dramatic presentations, concerts, displays, discussions of all kinds and at all levels by people from within and without the region. He must, by providing facilities and showing a sympathetic and informed interest, stimulate and encourage the formation of group activities of all kinds - from a study of medieval architecture to Scottish Country Dancing. He must enable his Youth Tutor to develop the area Youth Service to the full - not least by showing to sceptical elder citizens his belief in young people and in their value to the community. As supervisor of the branch library he must ensure that the librarian is able to provide a service as efficient as it is vital to a rural community. The Village College is a sub-office of the County Careers Advisory Service and the Warden, in consultation with the County Careers Advisory staff, must ensure that children leaving school, and young people who have left school, are placed in careers which will be satisfying to them and to their employers. The Village College is also licensed as a place of public entertainment and all applications for the hire of the premises and its facilities are referred to the Warden as licensee.* (Bowen 1973: 103 - 104)

By way of recompense Wardens received enhanced pay and free housing. Sawston's first Warden got £10 per annum to undertake the work of distributing unemployment insurance payments plus £50 for special responsibilities. They also enjoyed, although the brief presence of some indicates this was not always appreciated, the opportunity to be involved in one of the most exciting educational innovations of the moment. A chance to work in an institution basking in often quite novel local and national prestige; different, even exceptional for having dispelled the '*peculiarly adolescent ethos of the ordinary school*' (Farnell 1968: 103).

Inevitably Cambridgeshire attracted in addition to those recruited for the usual sweep of reasons, a mix of educational gold-diggers and idealists. The former transients assumed a brief residency would secure a valued imprimatur on their curriculum vitae, communicating the image of 'innovator', and negotiable for promotion elsewhere. The idealists often, with encouragement from Morris departed to spread the gospel elsewhere, but many once imbued with the ethos of service to the community stayed until retirement and beyond. Longevity bestowed benefits. Working in the Colleges offered the prestige of being associated with a distinctive institution, superior in so many ways to the traditional school; work in attractive and aesthetically pleasing surroundings; and an opportunity to immerse oneself within a community to an extent rarely extended to other teachers. It also meant being part of an institution young people enjoyed attending, where problems of vandalism and disruptive behaviour were apparently unknown (Farnell 1968: Dybeck 1981). They however posed atypical challenges which teachers were obliged to address. Farnell, who taught in a Village College, conveys some of these tensions as well as the sense of excitement and commitment, which many now recount with affection and sense of loss:

> *it is a job which spreads itself beyond working hours, into leisure hours, and into "private" daily life, for the public at large has definite and vigorously held views on how teachers should not only teach, but live. A teacher is called upon to exemplify in his personal life the norms of the society to which he belongs. There are obvious points of stress in such a situation: the teacher may hold values different from those society would have him pass on; he may feel the local community is making unreasonable demands on him; it may be that the teachers' disease, "status anxiety", afflicts him. Certainly, he has to establish a fine balance of classroom manner that maintains control, encourages learning, and elicits from his audience sympathy with those values he wishes to transmit. Role-conflict, insecurity, dissatisfaction, frustration can gnaw at the teacher's*

> *determination to give of his best, erode his authority and influence, and nudge off balance the quivering classroom-equilibrium. The Village College system complicates the situation. It is common to find the teacher living very close to the College. An uncommonly large number of the children he teaches know where he lives and are known by him. He sees them in the village with their parents and friends, at play or at work. It is likely he just happens to know their parents; but he may in fact teach them at night. It is possible he has in this same group his doctor, staff from the local junior school, the wives of a couple of school governors, one or two of his own colleagues, day scholars and ex-day scholars. His relationship with his position, his profession, his superiors, children, adult students, colleagues is intimately known - for no one should make the mistake of thinking all these people are not interested in such matters. They intrigue them. After evening classes he may call in at the local. There may be one or two in the local he does not personally know, but they know him. One or two of last year's fifth formers will be at the bar, and very likely one of this year's fifth form girls will be sitting demurely sipping in a corner. There is only one possible code of behaviour in the Village College situation. There is no room for playing a part, for posing as a unique authority, for assuming god-like righteousness, for wearing an aura of intellectual eminence, for Pharisaic apartheid. It is a very careful, stunted, and very likely tortured man who can cover himself with a cloak of falsehood in the Village College. The teacher in a Village College who uses only his sacrosanct position as his source of classroom authority is likely to find difficulty, as is the poseur, the bully, the sluggard, the snob, the pompous. But if a man reveals himself to be an intellectual, the luxury will be allowed him; a social recluse, his isolation will be respected; a man of dignity, so will he be treated; an entertainer, entertain he must. .... In reality, the strain of Village College life can be overwhelming.* (1968: 105 - 106)

The above was written as the 'golden age' of the Village College was drawing to a close. Certainly Ree reflecting on a tour of the Colleges in 1980 detected increasing inertia following the retirement of Morris and in some cases a conscious striving to jettison the founding principles. Growing teacher mobility; inter-college rivalry which generated an obsession with trivia and 'window-dressing'; mounting pressure from employers and parents for schooling to be focused on transferable skills and the acquisition of examination results, were trends already eroding the equilibrium of the Colleges by the 1970s. Similar yet more invasive trends were to follow.

Chapter Four

Final years

For a fleeting period, spanning the end of the War, Morris must have thought his 'Plan' was about to be translated into a national policy. Maxwell Fry, who collaborated with Gropius in seeing Impington through to completion, certainly judged it to have been *'formally adopted'* (1944: 90) by the government. Finally it seemed Village Colleges were being lauded as the saviour of rural education and Morris in their wake was emerging as a significant national figure. Collectively things looked rosy. During the parliamentary debate preceding the passing of the 1944 Education Act, the Minister singled out the Colleges for a special mention; the **British Way and Purpose** (Directorate of Army Education 1944) in its vision of the new post-war Britain specifically mentions the Colleges as a model to be emulated; and the influential Scott Committee on rural development proposed that *'steps should be taken to provide [in rural areas] social centres of the village college type'* (HMSO 1944: para 170). In 1945, Elmslie Philips, previously assistant to Morris but now Director of Education for Devon, published a development plan proposing the creation of units on the lines of the Village Colleges of Cambridgeshire. In 1948 his friend W J Deacon, Chief Officer of Somerset, published an ambitious scheme for 21 Village Colleges; and in 1947 Stewart Mason, bolstered by a glowing reference from Morris, secured the Directorship of Leicestershire and immediately began formulating plans for a *'series of community colleges based on the Cambridgeshire model'* (Jones 1988: 28). Simultaneously on a more personal level regular invitations came from the BBC to speak to foreign and British audiences. In particular, 1946 was a remarkable year. The Colonial Office asked him to visit West Africa for two months to report on the development of post school education; the Air Ministry appointed him a member the Educational Advisory Committee for the RAF; and to cap the lot, he was invited to become adviser for two days per week to Lewis Silkin, Minister of Town and Country Planning. Silkin, then supervising the New Town programme, the largest single building initiative ever undertaken in Britain specifically summoned Morris to advise the Ministry on 'cultural and community aspects' of New Town development.

Retrospectively this period is best viewed as an Indian Summer. By 1947 the Ministry of Education had published plans for the implementation of the Further Education elements of the 1944 Act (Ministry of Education 1947). Village Colleges secured only a passing mention, which was more than they did in the accompanying document on Secondary Education which disregarded them even in the section on 'country schooling' (Ministry of Education 1947a). Both self-evidently conveyed the message that the Colleges were not a 'preferred model'. Even the meagre discussion in the former demonstrated scant sympathy or understanding pointedly stressing that where schools and community centres shared the same site '*separate entrances*' were essential (1947: 79). Maybe if Butler, a Cambridge man, regular visitor to Impington and Member for a nearby Essex constituency, had remained Minister of Education when his Act was implemented things might have been different? But that cannot be assumed. Even as early as 1943 in a prophetic report on Village Colleges submitted to Chuter Ede, Butler's pedestrian deputy, an HMI concluded achievements disproportionately depended on recruiting the 'right sort' of person as Warden. The author felt it was

> *difficult to believe that the Headmaster of most elementary schools are suitable people to deal with adolescents, much less to solve the intricate and obstinate problems of adult education. On the other hand, it would seem a thousand pities not to bring these various branches of education into one beautiful and*

> *well-equipped building.* (quoted van der Eyken and Turner 1969: 171)

Although the HMI probably did not appreciate it he or she had aligned themselves with Grundtvig by arguing you had to change the teaching profession first if progressive reforms were to stand a chance. Morris would not have appreciated that one bit.

Unfortunately when the Village Colleges might, just might, have taken off Morris was physically too exhausted and unduly distracted by peripheral projects to aid the process. Sadly the hoped for influence and national prominence never really materialised. In the 1950s and 1960s, when for a time a new school was opening somewhere in Britain every three weeks, there was the chance a radically different type of educational institution to the traditional school might have been inaugurated. But for that to have happened it would have required a rejection of selection something that was never on the cards. As he feared the opportunity to create educational, cultural and community centres capable of providing for the whole person; of eroding the artificial age divisions Morris rightly perceived as bedevilling education; and build Colleges visibly demonstrating '*in stone the continuity and never ceasingness of education*' (Morris 1925: 11) was lost. Squandered also during this period was the unrepeatable opportunity to erect buildings that enhanced and adorned their environments. Morris once quoted a teacher representative who interjected at a planning meeting '*Mr Chairman, I hope that no aesthetic consideration will stand in the way of school buildings being put up rapidly after the war is over*' (Morris 1945: 104). Sadly the victory of such Philistines was virtually complete and rarely did the thousands of schools thrown-up during post-war years speak of anything apart from a parsimonious contempt for the visual arts. As he feared they would '*dullness and lack of vision*' prevailed. Few '*graced*' their surroundings, inspired students or provided a '*centre of reference arousing the affection and loyalty of the local population*' (1925: 9).

Little was accomplished during the time spent with the Ministry of Town and Country Planning. Few planners were sympathetic to either his ideas or presentational style. Even the Directors of Education in the areas where the New Towns were built found '*his idea of multidimensional complex catering for all ages and offering opportunities for recreation and study ... simply indigestible*' (Ree 1973: 115). This unhappy association, however, produced a paper prepared in March 1948 that translated his rural vision to an urban context. Based upon the assumption that each New Town would acquire a population of 60,000 plus it proposed that in addition to a central grouping there should be three campuses placed between the centre and the periphery serving approximately a third of the inhabitants. These were to be multi-purpose urban Village Colleges, Welfare and Community centres. Village Colleges on an unprecedented scale designed to draw people of all ages and backgrounds together. At the heart of the New Town itself was to be Morris's Bauhaus, or as he more mundanely designated it for the ears of English planners, a College of Further Education. Bearing scant relationship to the intellectually, aesthetically and fiscally impoverished institutions subsequently given that name it, like the Bauhaus itself founded by Gropius and his comrades, was where those from 'trades and callings' would go to collectively develop their skills and artistry. Where they might forge a creative bond between design, craftsmanship and industry. The College was to be

> *an important and significant part of the central square or squares, where the administrative and cultural should, so to speak, be blended. Thus there should be a close association between the College of Further Education, and the art gallery, the concert hall and the town's main library, all three of which will be conceived on livelier and more imaginative lines than in the past. These buildings should have some relation to the town's administrative centre, so that in the result education will not be separated from the active appreciation and practice of the Arts and all of them will not be entirely divorced from civic administration. One example of*

> *what might be aimed at is to be found in St Mark's Square at Venice with the Doge's Palace, the Cathedral, the Courts of Justice, the Library, Municipal Offices, etc., surrounding perhaps the most potent and moving space in Europe. The theatre has also to be remembered. There is no need to be dogmatic about the actual form of the location of these public buildings in addition to the law court and other administrative buildings. It is possible for them to be place in very significant relationship even if they are placed in two communicating squares or spaces. The important thing that has been said is to associate education with ordinary life and both with the practice of the Arts and with civic administration.* (Morris 1948: 120)

Morris was not alone in advocating such integration, of fusing social life and education. For example Roberts and Weaver in the **British Way and Purpose** (1944) stressed the benefits of building urban communities around their schools. Morris however envisaged far more. Not merely a community gathered for convenience around the local school, but an new educational institution catering for all which *'would lie athwart the daily lives of the community it served'* (1925: 11). Merely to visit the New Towns designed and built in the post-war period provides abundant evidence of the human and social costs that flowed from the obdurate refusal of planners and educators to follow his lead. Morris railed against those communities where ugliness is accepted as normal, beauty regarded as a luxury or even eccentric, he would be outraged by what he encountered if he toured those New Towns today.

The College of Further Education recommended to the New Town Development Corporations was based on his own Cambridgeshire Regional College of Technology and Design. This, perhaps his last great scheme, was to be built on a 48 acre site located on the outskirts of Cambridge. Council approval was given in July 1949 and Jack Howe, who worked with Fry and Gropius on Impington, was given the design brief. As with the Village Colleges Morris envisaged a scheme far in advance of anything then existing in Britain.

Indeed Howe was instructed to undertake a study visit to colleges in Sweden, Denmark, France and Switzerland to seek inspiration. Morris threw himself into planning what might have become a template for the polytechnics established in the 1960s. Alongside subjects already established in Technical Colleges were to be departments offering music and foreign languages. Also a School of Design providing courses in fine arts, ceramics, furniture design, sculpture, printing and industrial design; and a School of Building and Architecture with three year courses in architecture, town and country planning, civil engineering and landscape design. Residential accommodation for out-of-town students; a state of the art auditorium designed for public performances of plays, opera, concerts and films; theatre and music workshops; two gymnasia; and a swimming pool were also itemised in the brief. The detailed plans prepared by Morris and delivered to the Ministry of Education were in many respects as revolutionary as the Memorandum written two decades earlier. If the College had been erected it might have changed the ethos and direction of Further Education and possibly much of the Higher Education sector. Creating the model for a community university, similar to the American Land Grant universities, for which we have no precedent in the United Kingdom. Institutions designed to support via teaching and research their host communities, and to share with them the facilities and expertise at their disposal. It was not be, the Korean War and spending restrictions, along with an absence of governmental enthusiasm, did for it, and Morris now lacked the energy and autonomy to raise the funding as he had for the Village Colleges.

His final years in Cambridgeshire following the collapse of the Regional College scheme were an anti-climax. Towards the end he must have felt ground-down by austerity, exhaustion and Philistinism. Retirement came in 1954 shortly after Bassingbourn Village College, the sixth established during his tenure, opened. Four more were to be completed before he died in 1961. The inauguration of Comberton Village College in 1959 was the occasion of his last public appearance. By then he was a very sick man. Invited to perform the opening ceremony after a depressing, barely audible speech repeated three times the agony was eventually cut short when George Edwards, his successor, gently returned Henry to his seat.

Other Village Colleges opened during the next two decades but gradually the baton passed to areas such as Leicestershire and Coventry. Partially this was a consequence of Morris's policy of inviting up-and-coming young men (they were it seems always young men) to join him as trainees in his office or take posts in his Colleges. Such acolytes were then frequently encouraged to leave and spread the word elsewhere. As Ree (1973) shows this led to a complex network of 'old boys' scattered around the country in senior administrative, community education and teaching posts who had initially cut their teeth in Cambridgeshire. In this way the County lost many of the best and brightest amongst its recruits.

Morris, although physically absent, remained a potent figure within the County for sometime. As someone who worked on after Morris left recalls '*It must have been very difficult for Edwards who followed him. Long after he left the Education Department was overshadowed by him. There were devotees who could hardly utter a sentence without referring to him*'. Morris himself although increasingly frail devoted his remaining years to the development of two community projects. Hilltop in South Hatfield was a community centre built in a pub. Two breweries combined with the new Town Development Corporation to finance the project that, besides the usual pub facilities, possessed a restaurant, a hall for meetings, a number of committee rooms and a welfare clinic. At a time when any discussion regarding the presence of alcohol within community centres or schools invariably stirred up a hornets nest of controversy this was a radical departure. After a successful start the project foundered following a change of landlord and the links between the pub and community centre were largely severed.

Morris moved to a far more congenial project - Digswell Arts Trust, Welwyn. Displaying all the marks of his thinking not least a genuine spark of originality it was funded by a number of charitable trusts as well as the New Town Development Corporation. Digswell was in essence an artistic settlement. Artists were offered living and working accommodation in a converted manor house. This community of initially seven artists Morris envisaged would then take their respective talents out into the community beyond whilst attracting students and clients to Digswell. Morris saw the Centre as initiating a unique form of patronage in an age when the private patron was no longer commonplace. Trustees of the project included many who had been associated with Morris in the past including Herbert Read, Jack Pritchard, Nan Youngman and David Hardman. Living nearby the early success of Digswell and his close involvement undoubtedly gave him immense pleasure in his final years. He died in December 1961.

Chapter Five

Legacy

Maxwell Fry called Morris '*one of the most delicious English eccentrics he had ever met*' (MacCarthy 1984: 10). A description echoed by many. Less forthcoming are the numerous enemies left in his wake. Victims of a man who his heir tells us was '*unsurpassed in the techniques of calculated rebuke*' (Farnell 1968: 19) and who another colleague recalls '*was a vicious employer if he took against you*'. The majority seem to more fondly remember him as '*charming and delightful*', short tempered but '*so forgiving*' and '*a cross between an ogre and a saint*'. Few surely doubt he was a difficult man to work with. So intense was his affection for the Colleges staff lived with a constant threat of him 'dropping in' and taking umbrage at some slight to the building or guiding principle. One ex-Warden described Morris expressing irrational annoyance at the Autumn leaves blowing 'messily' around the College garden; a teacher recalls him walking into a hall and being so irritated by the poor quality of the choir rehearsal he snatched the baton from the member of staff and took charge. Another told of Morris appearing unheralded with a party of visitors at a College. Opting to include a staff house in the visit, he opened the door without knocking and embarked on a guided tour completely ignoring the occupants. Such behaviour ensured the intimate but fundamentally unstable relationship he shared with the Wardens could not continue uncontested. Even prior to his retirement it was apparent expansion in the number and size of the Colleges would weaken the centralised control he wielded. As this occurred so the Colleges one ex-Warden ruminated '*became more and more just like an ordinary school*', or in the words of a retired community tutor '*they simply regressed to the norm*'; until according to Dybeck they faded into '*a pale reflection of what might have been*' (1981: 7).

As with so many radical educational experiments from New Lanark, to Prestolee and beyond the unrelenting pressure to conform eventually shunted the Village Colleges into line. Yet they remain monuments to a magnificent dream. Compared to the dull tired utilitarian predictability of the bulk of school architecture they are an indictment of the pusillanimousness of those responsible for the post-war and earlier school-building programmes. Space, light and the air of permanence speak of a different concept of education to that conveyed by the off-the-peg designs prevailing elsewhere. Also the Village Colleges are a constant irritant, reminding us of a missed opportunity to bequeath to both town and country buildings with the capacity to convey the grandeur of architecture and the majesty of education. Unlike most schools in appearance they are more akin to a college than a factory unit; in this respect the judgement of an early American visitor still holds

> *No one can visit the Village Colleges without being impressed by the simple beauty, the high quality of the educational material used, and the intelligence and wisdom characterizing the whole undertaking.* (quoted by Dent 1943 :15)

Once inside however they are now in most respects a profound disappointment. A shadow of what might have been, not because they were badly built but because of the way they are now run. The balance is all wrong, the integration of old and young, the vision of service, are somehow missing. They sell a product to customers, take it or leave it, and those without cash are less and less welcome here, as elsewhere. Adult students and users are increasingly customers who today can no more presume collective ownership of the College than they can of the Barclays Bank down the road.

Morris understood that when an institution confines itself to the young and attendance is enforced by compulsion teachers will all too readily be seduced or obliged into adopting the persona of a *'pundit or a tyrant'* (1926: 42). Devoid of the essential checks and balances that Morris believed would prevent the historic pattern re-emerging the contemporary Village Colleges have reverted to type. No longer does the ogre from County Hall descend to control the dominance of the dominie, gone also is the intimacy, the openness described by Farnell which performed a similar function. They are a profound disappointment because they are so like other schools. Good schools certainly, but schools nevertheless. The mindless conformity of school uniforms; the relative scarcity of adults during weekdays; the ringing of bells announcing the onset and cessation of lessons; the demeanour of the 'teachers' - especially the unnatural, unwarranted deference accorded the 'Head' - along with the assumed superiority conveyed to the students; the predictability of the notice 'all visitors must report to reception' matched by the inquisitorial often menacing "can I help you?"; the break and lunch-time patrols; the ill-mannered interjection of the Warden disrupting your conversation with a member of 'their' staff to discover who this stranger 'in my school' is; the rehearsed homily delivered by the Warden in the dominant argot of their kind, mixing Charles Handy management speak with Forest Gump aphorisms, followed by hurried excuses predicating a departure which informs you what you already knew - namely you are neither rich enough nor sufficiently influential to be worth dallying with; all these and so much else confirm the first impression - these are schools no longer Colleges. Better schools than average in most respects but schools nevertheless - no longer Countryman's Colleges. Sadly you sense Morris would now also judge his Village Colleges despite his tireless efforts to have descended to the rank of *'bloody schools'*.

Even during the early stages critics questioned the merits of his project. Edwards-Rees (1944), an influential youth work practitioner, believed the Colleges, if successful, would prove *'a deathblow'* to the spiritual and corporate life of villages. Their lavish facilities and equipment, as transport improved, acting as a *'magnet'* emptying surrounding villages and hamlets. She pressed for investment in the small communities so they might have at their core a '*homely pub*', junior school, nursery and hall with '*two or three rooms for groups of all ages and a special room for young people*' (ibid: 93). Peers (1958: 93) an Adult Educator was equally suspicious. Arguing there was no evidence even institutions as '*admirably planned*' as the Colleges would overcome the inherent problems emanating from a mixing of adolescents and adults. Peers was probably mistaken in that the Colleges for a period seemed to have shown that where the will to do so existed then generations can profitably be blended. According to Edwards-Rees the movement towards centralisation embodied in the Morris Plan was '*happily foredoomed to failure, for the village tradition is still strong enough to defeat it*' (1944: 93). She was right in her assessment of Morris, he was an unashamed centralizer. G K Chesterton once said of Bernard Shaw that he saw modern society not as an unrighteous kingdom but as an untidy room. Morris likewise was desperate to tidy up and sort out the room. However she was completely wrong when it came to the capacity of the village to resist the blandishments of the Colleges and the nearest urban centre. Much as Morris was erroneous in his belief the Colleges could accomplish the reconstruction of a rural way of life. Returning today he would be delighted (even surprised) by the prosperity of Cambridgeshire. The Colleges may have contributed in some way but it would be exceedingly difficult to quantify such a claim. Not least because similar affluence is to be found elsewhere in once poor rural counties which never had Village Colleges or anything approaching them. By his retirement in 1954 it must have been apparent that whatever his achievements, and they were many, neither he nor anyone else could save the English village from being over-run by the urban juggernaut. Melbourn Village College, opened two years prior to his death, contains within its catchment area Foxton village. Parker's history of Foxton concludes with an evocative epitaph for a lost world, it helps summarise why in this respect the Colleges failed, but were preordained to do so:

> *Then, gradually at first but with ever-increasing momentum, came the social avalanche which swept away the last traces of 'village life' and transformed life for everybody, everywhere. For the first time in this book I am able to give credit to politicians and planners, and I do it unreservedly - for the 1944 Education Act and subsequent legislation which has brought about a huge expansion in secondary and higher education; for the Social Security plan which did more to abolish poverty in ten years than Poor Laws had done in four hundred years; for Town and Country Planning, Housing Authorities, Health Services, etc. All this, in conjunction with paid holidays, higher wages, cheaper travel, cars by the million, air-travel, television and a host of electrical gadgets in the home, this is what I mean by the avalanche that swept away 'village life'. There is no point whatever in talking any longer about 'village life' and 'town life'. It is just life.* (Parker 1976: 265)

Morris could hardly have been expected in 1924 to have predicted changes of that order.

It is tempting to paint a picture of failure. Even Digswell has gone. Broken up into 'yuppie flats' and none of the present occupants I accosted had heard of Morris and only one couple had any inkling it had once housed a unique experiment in community arts. Visiting Digswell today like touring the Village Colleges can be a melancholy experience. In the decades since Ree revisited Cambridgeshire the proclivity, he observed, of those running the Colleges to turn *'their backs on the hopes and ideals of the originator'* (Ree 1980) seems to have gathered pace. Commencing with Sawston in 1993 a growing number of Colleges have become GM (grant maintained). Opting out to better quarantine themselves from both the influence of elected councillors, the LEA and the local community. Opting instead to relate to parents as customers not as citizens and by their selfishness doing so much to demolish the very local democracy they were in part created to enrich. Consequently the Heads of these new GM schools according to Barker are inclined to *'operate in isolation from the common cause'* and narrow their loyalties to *'a single, small institution'* (1997: 32). Some have contemplated deleting "Village" from the title whilst retaining the apparently prestigious College with its snobbish Public School connotations. One local authority officer mentioned how Henry *'is now barely recalled or remembered nowadays'*. Yet on the wider stage Morris has not been entirely forgotten or his thinking rejected. The Memorandum still retains the capacity to inspire those reading it for the first time as those of us who have used it for teaching purposes well know. Like others who strove to create educational institutions concerned with *'the whole welfare of communities'* (Morris 1926) his name may currently be less frequently invoked than previously. But his ideas survive, in part because the Village Colleges convinced a generation of educational reformers that the 'community school' was achievable. As Herbert Read enthused after visiting Impington

> *Is it possible, not merely to conceive, but to build and introduce into the existing educational system, schools which provide the essentials of an educative environment? The answer is yes; it has been done in at least one instance (Impington), and a model perhaps not perfect in every detail, but practical, functional and beautiful, does exist on English soil.* (Read 1958: 136)

In recent years the community school has enjoyed something of a comeback. Third Way theorists and communitarians are keen on using schools, not this time in order to compensate for the declining influence of the Church but to counter the collapse of 'family values' and regulate the underclass. Sadly their community schools are motivated by fear of an old enemy 'the proles' not a love of life. School days along with the school years are being extended to the point when young people are left with little time to experience life beyond the classroom and the television. Parental involvement, but rarely if ever the involvement of other adults, is being raised to the status of an unquestioned good. Bringing parents in from the school gate being hailed as a sign we are moving towards a new era in community schooling. It is nothing of the kind. Parents along with carefully screened representatives from community are however simply being assigned the role of handmaiden to the teachers who need all the help they can get in their quest to achieve the ever more outlandish outputs and targets set by an ever more authoritarian central government. These modern 'community schools' are almost exclusively concerned with the young. Therefore as Morris forewarned they impose a childish world on young people and teachers alike encouraging *'a disproportionate emphasis on methods of imparting information and the intensive analysis of the subject-matter curricula'* (1926: 37). Providing a shallow, limited and emasculate version of the 'educative environment' Read saw developing within the Village Colleges. As literacy and numeracy hours drive out history, music and the liberal arts; and the obsession with targets inspires a 'serious' debate in the United States about the benefits of removing playgrounds from schools sites (they encourage the wrong frame of mind by encouraging young people to think of schools as places of enjoyment), so it becomes ever more obvious that in the present climate schools will not be transformed into *'microcosms of life and places of liberal culture'*. Rather like the schools of death Grundtvig feared they will, as Morris told us they would if education was not shaped by a philosophy of life, become ever more divorced *'from creation of all kinds, from play and love and tragedy, from religion and art and discourse'* (ibid: 38).

Morris would have been comfortable with the contemporary pessimism prevailing amongst progressive educationalists. Indeed he continuously returns to the theme of cultural collapse believing he dwelt in a period *'a vast cultural breakdown'* evident in the decline of the *'visual environment'* (1945: 103). Equally he would be no more impressed by the schools of today than he was with those of the 1920s. The strap, cane and slap may have disappeared from our schools thanks to European legislation. Classes are smaller, classrooms better furnished, more pupil friendly but in so many ways things remain unchanged. The subjects comprising the National Curriculum barely differ from those of the Revised Code he grew up with. Then as now teachers are subjected to aggressive bullying metered out by unsympathetic inspectors, required to deliver an imposed curriculum, judged by their capacity to impose passivity in the classroom and the marks achieved by their pupils in tests. The buildings are better but the cultural and intellectual vacuum at the core remains intact.

When entering schools count the certificates, tot up the awards and survey the photographs. Look at the people pictured on them. Never artists, authors, musicians or creative souls; certainly never philosophers or educationalists. Overwhelmingly you confront the smug grins of the men and women drawn from the local business community. Petty Poujadists and overweight underlings from the Public Relations Department presenting cheques (for trifling amounts) and certificates (for trivial achievements) to grinning pupils and deferential teachers. Sometimes to ring the changes the pictures feature minor politicians, TV 'stars' of the most inconsequential kind (weathermen or local newsreaders) or sports personalities without personalities wallowing in another fleeting moment of adulation. Besides them trivial certificates and trifling awards dispensed by organisations few have heard of and even fewer must care about. Art driven out by the baubles and trinkets collected and dispensed by sad men and women desperate to have their efforts validated by someone, anyone in authority.

In an age of imperialism, head teachers reached unerringly for the military metaphor to validate their contribution. As befitted the greatest naval power in the world it was usually a naval one. They were the captain, keeping a firm hand on the tiller, a weather eye open for trouble, never sailing too close to the wind and above all maintaining a tight ship. Today with a similar lack of imagination in an age when multi-nationals rule the metaphors, the language imitates the worlds of business and high finance. The style is similarly fraudulent and now as then belies a serious absence of educational and cultural depth. Lacking in many cases a grasp of even the first or even second principles of education they embezzle from elsewhere a language and imagery to explain to themselves and others what they do and what they seek to achieve. Morris would, I suspect, have had scant tolerance for such charlatans.

The enemies that Morris faced-down were the landowner and parson who for selfish reasons denied generations of countrymen and women a half-decent education. Today the threat emerges from a different quarter. In an age when business is securely in the saddle it emanates from those seeking compliant workers and submissive consumers. Who desire nothing more, as Morris warned us they would, than to see '*the majority are half-educated, and many not even a quarter-educated, and where large fortunes and enormous power can be obtained by exploiting ignorance and appetite*' (1945: 103). Rapidly we are seeing the governance of education drifting ever further away locally elected officials and educationalists and into the grasp of central government and via them into the hands of business organisations, tycoons and their nominees. Already 'for profit' organisations are running schools in the United States and elsewhere, now those self same organisations are actively lobbying to extend their operations in Britain. Their jurisdiction has to be resisted as doggedly as that of the parson, squire and factory owner of the past. Morris never believed that those who owned the country should govern it. He opposed them because the covert aspiration of such individuals and groups is always to manipulate education in order to better limit intellectual and religious freedom, stifle autonomous associations, and ensure our educational institutions serve their narrow ends rather than those of the wider community and the student. The new overseers, like their predecessors manifest the same scant desire to create an education system devoted to the '*pursuit of goodness, of truth, of beauty*' (Morris 1946: 109). Which is why Morris rightly feared any structure not based on a recognition that '*the proper architects of education are philosophers, artists, scientists, prophets and scholars, operating in freedom*' (1941a: 71)

It is important to perpetually expose the limits of an education system based, like ours, on opportunism rather than truth. To highlight the dangers posed by a system dominated by a desire to manipulate the young so they meekly fit into the established order and which has no desire to prepare them for a life truly worth living. That seeks at every turn to encourage accommodation and conformity rather than offer young and old the chance to encounter truth, justice and what in conversation Morris frequently characterised as the '*dignities of education*'. Such a magnificent expression, it captures so richly what Henry Morris indefatigably toiled to accomplish and what is still absent from our current education system. Protecting, extending and extolling those '*dignities of education*' was no simple task during the lifetime of Morris and has not become less exacting since his passing but there surely cannot be any higher pursuit. But pursuit it will always be for as he warned us in the world of '*values victory is never won once and for all ... freedom has to be won daily*' (Morris 1946: 109). Indeed.

Bibliography

Ashbee, C. R. (1914) *The Hamptonshire Experiment in Education*, George Allen.

Baker, W. P. (1953) *The English Village*, Oxford University Press.

Barker, B. (1997) 'Who Killed the Local Education Authority - Cambridgeshire 1974-1998? *Cambridge Journal of Education 27(1).*

Barnett, H. (1919) *Canon Barnett, His Life, Work and Friends*, Houghton Mifflin.

Barnett, H. and Barnett, S. (1901) *Towards Social Reform*, Fisher Unwin.

Begtrup, H., Lund, H. and Manniche, P. (1936) *The Folk High Schools of Denmark*, Humphrey Milford.

Bonham-Carter, V. (1971) *The Survival of the English Countryside*, Hodder and Stoughton.

Bowen, F. Watson (1973) 'The Cambridgeshire Village College: A Cultural Centre for Village Life' *Aspects of Education* pp 98-110.

Bracey, H. C. (1959) *English Rural Life: Village Activities, Organisations and Institutions*, Routledge and Kegan Paul.

Burr, W. (1929) *Small Towns: An Estimate of their Trade and Culture*, Macmillan.

Burton, H. M. (1943) *The Education of the Countryman*, Routledge and Kegan Paul.

Carson, M. (1990) *Settlement Folk*, University of Chicago Press.

Davies, N. (1931) *Education for Life: A Danish Pioneer*, Williams Norgate.

Decker, L. E. (1972) *Foundations of Community Education*, Pendell.

Dent, H. C. (1943) *The Countryman's College*, Longmans.

Dent, H. C. (1946) *Education in Transition*, Routledge and Kegan Paul.

Dewey, J. (1899) *The School and Society*, University of Chicago Press.

Dewey, J. (1902) 'The School As Social Center' in *Yearbook of the National Society for the Study of Education* University of Chicago Press.

Directorate of Army Education (1944) *The British Way and Purpose* War Office.

Duncan, J. (1938) *Mental Deficiency*, Watts.

Dybeck, M. (1981) *The Village College Way*, Cambridgeshire County Council.

Edwards (1974) *The Burston School Strike*, Lawrence and Wishart.

Edwards-Rees, D. (1944) *A Rural Youth Service* Methodist Youth Department.

Eggleston, J. D. and Bruere, R. W. (1913) *The Work of the Community School* Harper and Brothers.

Evans, W. W. (1921) 'Community Service of the Democratized Rural School' in *Yearbook of the National Society for the Study of Education*, University of Chicago Press.

Eyken, W. van der and Turner, B. (1969) *Adventures in Education*, Allen Lane.

Farnell, D. (1968) *Henry Morris: An Architect of Education*, Unpublished Thesis Cambridge Institute of Education.

Fenn, T. (undated) *Recalling Henry Morris 1889-1961*, Private.

Foght, H. W. (1915) *Rural Denmark and its Schools*, Macmillan.

Foght, H. W. (1918) *The Rural Teacher and His Work*, Macmillan.

Fry, E. Maxwell (1944) '*School Buildings*' in R A Scott-James (ed) *Education in Britain: Yesterday, To-day, To-morrow* Frederick Muller.

Gluek, E. T. (1927) *Community Use of Schools*, Williams and Wilkin.

Gordon, P. and White, J. (1979) *Philosophers as Educational Reformers: The influence of idealism on British educational thought and practice*, Routledge and Kegan Paul.

Green, T. H. (1888) *Collected Works Vol 3*, Longmans.

Hacker, L. W. (1929) 'The County-Community School Unit in Illinios' *American School Board Journal (78).*

Haggard, H. (1911) *Rural Denmark and Its Lessons*, Longman, Green.

Hardie, J. L. (1946) *Education and the Community*, Art and Educational Publishers.

HMSO (1942) *Report of the Committee on Land Utilisation in Rural Areas (The Scott Committee)* Cmd 6378. HMSO.

Himmelfarb, G. (1995) *The De-moralization of Society: From Victorian Virtues to Modern Values*, IEA Books.

Humphries, S. (1981) *Hooligans or Rebels? An Oral History of Working Class Childhood and Youth*, Blackwell.

Hurt, J. S. (1979) *Elementary Schooling and the Working Classes 1860-1918*, Routledge and Kegan Paul.

Joad, C. E. M. (1945) *About Education*, Faber.

Jones, D. (1988) *Stewart Mason: The Art of Education*, Lawrence and Wishart.

Jones, H. (1919) *The Principles of Citizenship*, Macmillan.

Koch, H. (1952) *Grundtvig*, Antioch Press.

Lerner, R. M. (1996) *America's Youth in Crisis: Challenges and Options for Programs and Policies*, Sage.

MacCarthy, F. (1984) 'Introduction' to J Pritchard *View from a Long Chair: the memoirs of Jack Pritchard*, Routledge and Kegan Paul.

MacCunn, J. (1907) *Six Radical Thinkers*, Arnold.

Manniche, P. (1939) *Denmark: A Social Laboratory*, Humphrey Milford.

Martin, E. W. (1965) *The Shearers and the Shorn: A Study of Life in a Devon Community*, Routledge and Kegan Paul.

Ministry of Education (1947) *Further Education*, HMSO.

Ministry of Education (1947a) *The New Secondary Education*, HMSO.

Moller, J. C. and Watson, K. (1944) *Education in Democracy: The Folk High Schools of Denmark*, Faber.

Morris, H. (1924) *The Village College. Being a Memorandum on the Provision of Educational and Social Facilities for the Countryside, with Special Reference to Cambridgeshire*, Cambridge County Council (reprinted in Ree 1984 and Dybeck 1981).

Morris, H. (1925) *The Village College. Being a Memorandum on the Provision of Educational and Social Facilities for the Countryside, with Special Reference to Cambridgeshire*, CUP (reprinted in Ree 1973 and Dybeck 1981).

Morris, H. (1926) 'Institutionalism and Freedom in Education' *New Ideals Quarterly 2(i).*

Morris, H. (1941) 'The Danish High School Myth' *Adult Education* pp 76-79.

Morris, H. (1941a) *Post War Policy in Education*, paper to Association of Directors and Secretaries of Education (reprinted Ree 1984).

Morris, H. (1945) *Buildings for Further Education*, paper Royal Institute of British Architects (reprinted Ree 1984).

Morris, H. (1946) *Liberty and the Individual,* talk given on BBC Home Service (reprinted Ree 1984).

Morris, H. (1948) *Education, Community Centre and Other Cultural Institutions,* paper prepared for Development Corporations (reprinted Ree 1984).

Morris, H. (1956) *Architecture, Humanism and the Local Community,* Paper Royal Institute of Architects (reprinted Ree 1984).

Nettleship, R. L. (1888) *Memoir of T H Green* in Collected Works of T H Green, Longmans.

Newby, H. (1980) *The Deferential Worker,* Allen Lane.

Palmer, M. (1976) 'Henry Morris' *Education* 12th March.

Parker, R. (1976) *The Common Stream,* Paladin.

Peers, R. (1958) *Adult Education: A Comparative Study,* Routledge and Kegan Paul.

Perry, C. A. (1910) *Wider Use of the School Plant,* Russell Sage.

Pevsner, N. (1954) *Cambridgeshire: The Buildings of England (10)*
Pritchard, J (undated) *Recalling Henry Morris 1889-1961,* Private.

Punke, H. (1951) *Community Uses of Public School Facilities,* King's Crown Press.

Rashdall, H. (1895) *Universities of Europe in the Middle Ages,* OUP.

Rashdall, H. (1902) 'The Functions of a University in a Commercial Centre' *Economic Review* January.

Read, H. (1958) *Education Through Art,* Faber.

Ree, H. (1973) *Educator Extraordinary: The Life and Achievement of Henry Morris,* Longman.

Ree, H. (1980) 'A Case of Arrested Development' *TES* 17th October.

Ree, H. (1990) 'Still haunted by Morris's ghost' *TES* 27th April.

Roberts, E. and Weaver, T. (1944) 'Education and the Citizen' in Directorate of Army Education *The British Way and Purpose*, War Office.

Robertson Scott, J. W. (1925) *England's Green and Pleasant Land* Cape.

Rordam, T. (1965) *The Danish Folk High Schools*, Det Danske Selskab.

Rowntree, B. S. and Lavers, G. (1951) *English Life and Leisure*, Longmans.

Sadler, M. (1926) *'Introduction'* H. Begtrup, H. Lund and P. Manniche (1935) *The Folk High Schools of Denmark*, Humphrey Milford.

Saville, J. (1957) *Rural Depopulation in England and Wales 1851-1951*, Routledge and Kegan Paul.

Scanlon, D. (1959) 'Historical Roots for the Development of Community Education' N. B. Henry (ed.) *Community Education: Principles and Practices from World Wide Experience - The Fifty-Eighth Yearbook of the National Society for the Study of Education*, University of Chicago Press.

Schairer, R. (1937) *'Denmark: An example of the intensive education of a people'* H. V. Usill (ed.) *The Year Book of Education*, Evans.

Sharp, T. (1940) *Town Planning*, Pelican Books.

Sherman, H. C. (1944) *Adult Education for Democracy*, WEA.

Shute, C. (1998) *Edmond Holmes and 'The Tragedy of Education'*, Educational Heretics Press.

Simkhovitch, M. (1904) *'The Enlarged Function of the Public School'* National Conference of Charities and Correction Record pp 471-486.

Simkhovitch, M. (1938) *Neighborhood: My Story of Greenwich House*, Norton.

Stephenson, F. and Stephenson, G. (1942) *Community Centres: A Survey*, Community Centres Joint Research Committee.

Stewart, W. A. C. (1972) *Progressives and Radicals in English Education 1750-1970*, Kelley.

Stillman, C. G. and Cleary, R. Castle (1949) *The Modern School*, Architectural Press.

Thaning, K. (1972) *N F S Grundtvig*, Det Danske Selskab.

Vincent, A. and Plant, R. (1984) *Philosophy, Politics and Citizenship: The Life and Thought of the British Idealists*, OUP.

Vogt, P. L. (1917) *An Introduction to Rural Sociology*, Appleton.

Ward, C. (1980) 'Schools of Freedom' *The Raven (10)*.

Whitehouse, J. H. (1908) *The Next Step in the Reform of the Elementary School* The Toynbee Record.

Wise, M. (1931) *English Village Schools*, Hogarth Press.

Woods, A. (1920) *Educational Experiments in England*, Methuen

Woods, R. A. (1923) *The Neighborhood in Nation-Building*, Houghton, Mifflin.

Other books by Educational Heretics Press

A.S.Neill:'bringing happiness to some few chidren' £8-95

John Holt (paperback at £10-95) (hardback at £17-95)

Edmond Holmes: the tragedy of education' £7-95

Margaret McMillan: 'I learn, to succour the helpless' £7-95

Alice Miller: unkind society, parenting, schooling £7-95

Robert Owen: 'schooling the innocents' £7-95

The Next Learning System:
and why home-schoolers are trailblazers £7-95

Rules Routines and Regimentation:
young children reporting on their schooling £8-95

Participation, Power-sharing and
School Improvement £9-95

Parenting Without God:
experiences of a Humanist mother £7-95

Finding Voices, Making Choices:
the Communty Arts Workers £9-95

The Holistic Educators £7-95

Small Schools and Democratic Practice £7-95

Compulsory Schooling Disease £6-95

Theory and Practice of Regressive Education £7-95

Freethinkers' Guide to the Educational Universe
(Collection of quotations on education) £12-50

Freethinkers' Pocket Directory to the Educational
Universe £7-95